Now I Have the Best Job in the World

How God Helped Me through Sabotage in the Workplace

Mary V. Pate

References:
US Equal Employment Opportunity Commission
Department of Labor – Wages & Hours
HelpGuide.org Feb. 2013
Merriam-Webster Online Dictionary
Notes to Myself Page – My Signature Page for my Readers Notes.
ISBN-10: 069221822X
ISBN-13: 9780692218228
Library of Congress Control Number: 2014905245
Mary Pate, Laurel Springs, NJ

In Him also we have obtained an inheritance, being predestined according to the purpose of Him who works all things according to the counsel of His will, that we who first trusted in Christ should be to the praise of His glory.

Ephesians 1:11-12

Contents

Contents 2

Acknowledgements

I am acknowledging the people who have entered my life during this mandate and preordination by God to fulfill His purpose through me to benefit others, and to glorify God.

I am humbled with sincere thanks to the publishing and editing staff at Create Space for assisting me in getting this work completed. I would not have been able to do it without them.

I express my sincere love and gratitude to my family members who stood by me during those turbulent times.

The Holy Spirit strategically orchestrated my every move, every door opened or closed, and every person I encountered for any length of time was prearranged by Him. His word is truth. My sincere gratitude to Him for being the best teacher and friend I have ever had.

Introduction

This book is derived from years of living the American dream. I had been employed at one of the largest corporations in the US after leaving high school, and remained there for many years until an opportunity knocked and I decided to become the entrepreneur I always wanted to be. I soon became the owner and operator of a temporary employment agency. I loved what I did, because it gave me great satisfaction to be able to help others become employed, put food on their tables, and take care of their children. This is basically the bear minimum of living and taking care of your responsibilities in society.

The recession of the 1990's greatly affected the operations of my business, and after ten years I closed the agency. Thereafter, my life began to go on a serious roller coaster ride of being trapped in times of no employment. Over time, changing life styles from living well financially, to sometimes having no money was very difficult. I tried several times to return to the business world, but that was a difficult task to say the least. Thereafter, I began seeking employment in various companies, and it became a nightmare. I began to encounter the attitudes and mannerisms of people at some of these companies like nothing I had ever experienced before.

Simultaneously, the Lord began to call me into ministry. I had always attended church and loved what the bible offered me; however, during that time, I was not living my life fully and applying the word of God as I should have been. It was hard enough trying to survive on a daily basis, and suddenly, I had something else to contend with that was unfamiliar to me, and no one to talk to about it.

However, it was an opportune time for God to begin walking me into my purposed plan life. As a matter of fact the life I originally planned had nothing to do with being in ministry.

He allowed me to go through this for many years, while introducing me to the ministry world and my gifts, hearing his voice, and then moving me to step out in great faith. For more than six years, I had been living through some of my trials and tribulations of losing employment and fighting for my life. It was not that I couldn't do better; but whenever I tried, I couldn't seem to get back on track. No matter how many times I asked Him why I was enduring so much pain, He did not answer.

This book will take you on the journey I have traveled, becoming jobless and being sabotaged many times on some of those jobs, and the unclean spirits I encountered during the many years I traveled through the wilderness. Then in year 2000, the Lord spoke to me and said, "Write a book." Instantly, I knew He was speaking of writing a book about the circumstances I was living through. It had been thirteen years since His requests, and it took Him ten of those years before He spoke and gave me the title for the book.

Listed below are ten points that I hope you will receive while reading my book, and by all means get as much as you need.

1) Become more knowledgeable of methods used to sabotage persons in the workplace.
2) Familiarize yourself with unclean spirits and how they manifest in our character and the state of mind we develop overtime.
3) If you can't do it alone, seek help to free yourself of unclean spirits
4) Understand the actual scenarios that are used in my story because it is my life, and the Holy Spirit is the one who orchestrates my life.
5) Know that when God has a call on your life, He demands the truth to be told, not to hurt anyone, but people are the stories.

All the priests and prophets had work to do, and the people made up their stories.

6) Acknowledge and understand the seven spirits of God, and their importance.
7) Understand the purpose and plan God has for your life, and although it may look strange to others, it's your journey.
8) Build a relationship with the Father, Son and Holy Spirit and learn to hear their voices.
9) Learn to walk in His will and His way
10) Stay focused, and no matter what happens, love yourself.

Your spiritual "gifts" are to be used for God.

1

Mandated and Preordained

There is no better timing than God's timing. If you learn to live by His timing, you will never miss whatever He has for you.

The Lord spoke to me in the year 2000 and said, "Write a book." The revelation I received from Jesus was to write about being fired from several jobs prior to year 2000. At that moment, I realized that in seven years I had been terminated three times from previous jobs. I was just terminated from the third job, and was crying out to the Lord because I did not understand why this was happening to me. During the years of owning an employment agency, I had employed many people, which is why I found it so difficult upon trying to retain employment. But, after closing the business, things began to go terribly wrong.

When I began this book, I tried many times to give it a title and finish writing it. The title would not come to mind for many years, and neither did the completed work. In the year 2010 while sitting in a noonday church service, the Lord spoke and said, "Best Job in the World." I immediately knew He was speaking to me regarding the name of the book. The Lord had to take me through many pitfalls, losing more jobs, being busted and disgusted, and finally launching me into ministry before He revealed the title to me.

Finally, during all the teachings, the experiences in writing other books, and understanding the unclean spirits I have encountered, everything has been revealed through the name of Jesus. However, there was more to come before the process of losing jobs would be completed.

On another occasion in 2014, while in meditation, the Lord spoke to me and said, "This book is a mandate on your life preordained by God to be written by you." *A mandate is like an official command or a go-ahead. Something that is preordained is certain to happen and cannot be changed, especially because it has been decided by God.*

I actually asked God why He was allowing me to go through so much turmoil for many years, but I never received an answer until that moment. As always when I hear that sweet, still voice, I am the happiest woman in the world. I, like so many others before me was chosen to travel through trials, tribulations and tests to fulfill God's mandate on our lives, to benefit others and to glorify God. During the past years, I never thought of my losses as a mandate on my life and preordained by God until the very end. Then, I knew there was so much more to this than I originally understood. It is one thing when you know something, but it takes you to a whole different level when God reveals it to you. I am still baffled that He chose me to do a "special, unprecedented" job for Him. Still in awe although the task associated with the journey was extremely difficult.

To assist you in understanding the importance of my life having a mandate on it and was preordained by God, we will return to the word of God, where we will find many prophets and priests who also had mandates to fulfill God's purpose. This was also a command from God that morning as He said, "Show the people three others in the Bible who also had mandates and preordinations on their lives to give your readers more understanding of your walk with me." The list could be numerous; however, I am giving you a glimpse to educate you on various ways God uses the "called ones" for specific jobs to help build His kingdom.

Abraham and Sarah

The main story of Genesis was God's plan to bless all nations through Abraham's descendants, and for God's call to Abraham and Sarah to become the parents of new people, a new nation. This new nation would become God's tool for blessing all peoples. Although Abraham and Sarah were elderly, God chose to begin His plan of redemption for the entire world with them. Central to God's blessing was His covenant with Abraham, the Abrahamic Covenant. God, the awesome Creator of the entire universe, freely chose to make everlasting promises to Abraham and his descendants. These promises in the Abrahamic Covenant were the foundation for all of God's subsequent promises and covenants to the Bible. Genesis is not merely a beginning; it provides the foundation for the rest of the biblical narrative.

One of the reasons I love the Abraham story is because it led us into the beginning of time. Eventually the Gentiles received the same promises and privileges that the Israelites received being God's people. The Gentiles need to say "thank you" to the Israelites for being disobedient because it gave us freedom.

Moses

While Moses took the Israelites through the wilderness, and all the crosses he had to bear, he walked in the will and way of God. God first saved the infant Moses from a watery death and then provided him with the best education in the ancient world (–) Pharaoh's court. God later shaped Moses into an instrument for saving His people, the Israelites, from slavery. Moses spent 40 years wandering the wilderness trying to lead the Israelites out because they were God's people. It was supposed to have taken the Israelites eleven days to get to the Promised Land, but because of their disobedience, it took them forty years. But God was always their Savior. God used Moses at the opening of the Red Sea to save the Israelites from the power of the Egyptian army. Moses wrote the Ten Commandments for God. God used Moses to execute His many signs and wonders, and so much more while dealing with people who murmured and complained. Through all his trials and tribulations, Moses finally got the Israelites to the Promised Land; however, he did not go over himself. There's a great lesson to be learned whenever we are disobedient to God.

The Moses story is one that is very dear to my own heart because for seven years God called me on the mountain top to meet with Him.

I know it seems somewhat strange, but, He called me just like He did with Moses. Many times, I would feel His presence upon my spirit, and I would later meet Him on the mountaintop to listen for His instructions, read my bible, walk and talk with Him, and of course, pray. During one period of time, every Sunday morning for four weeks, He would not allow me to go to my home church because His call beckoned me to spend Sunday mornings with Him. On that mountaintop is where I totally submitted myself to Him. I screamed through the tall green trees, the sun shining down upon my face as I looked up into the sky; I only heard the wind in the trees, my voice screaming and crying in submission. At that moment, I promised Him that I would go wherever He wanted me to go, and do whatever He wanted me to do. I remember looking around and there was no one on the mountaintop but God and me. After that encounter, He released me to return to my home church, but not for long.

Jeremiah

God spoke to Jeremiah early on when he was just a youth and told him:

"Before I formed you in the womb I knew you; Before you were born I sanctified you; I ordained you a prophet to the nations."

Jeremiah 1:5.

Jeremiah was keenly aware that the call of God on his life had been determined by God from before his conception. As God's word became a reality in his life, the prophet understood that God ***knew*** *him and had called him to proclaim a critical message at a crucial point in the history of the nation. The word knew refers to an intimate knowledge that comes from relationship and personal commitment. That intimate relationship was made apparent in God's sanctifying work, whereby Jeremiah was "set apart" (made holy) for special service.* Jere*miah's role was to be a prophet to the nation of Judah as well as a messenger of God for all nations. Jeremiah serves to this day as an example of someone who remained faithful to the word of God despite countless hardships.*

Jeremiah often cried for the people, the nation and for himself during the time he served the Lord. This showed the compassion he had for the people and the faithfulness he had for the Lord, and living up to the call on His life. One of the ways I relate to Jeremiah's story is during the times of weeping. The Lord also instilled this pressure upon me as I often cried for others as He began to show me their hearts. Many times, others around me would call me "Jeremiah the crying prophet." In the beginning stages of my weeping, I didn't understand why I was crying, and wondered why the Lord thought I was always sad. However, He later told me that I cried when I encountered certain people because I was able to discern their hearts, and some of them were sad and hurting. Unfortunately, I still do this sometimes, and it's no fun.

There are some of us who have mandates on our lives to serve God in many ways, and when that time comes, we know that our faithfulness to His word is the ultimate despite any type of hardships we encounter.

Everyone has a testimony, and sometimes I felt like **Job** going through one trial after another wondering why God was allowing these fates to be against me. My life began to spiral downward in such a way that I went through peaks and valleys that spelled "unemployed" on my forehead. At various times, I would question "Where is my Jesus?" "Father, if this is not your will, please past this cup from me." It must have been His will, because this trauma went on, and got worse for many years. The ups and downs, the struggles, and the unbelievable madness continued. As fate would have it, keeping a job was unheard of for me; amid all the terminations, and abusive treatment from some of my former employers, I was having a very unfulfilling life, and I still didn't understand the reason behind it all. I thought it was very strange that after many years of employing others, and when I needed help, the wheels changed.

Remember, while you are traveling through your trials and tribulations, God will test you to see if you are getting what He is trying to teach you. If you fail the test, don't fret, God will give you another chance. Get up, repent, ask God for forgiveness, thank Him and try again. He said in His word, "He will never leave you nor forsake you," nor should you lean on your own understanding. Jehovah Shammah is there for you.

I knew there was a reason for all this, but did not understand the "what and whys" in God's way of doing things. I didn't understand at first that it all had to do with my future life, and the big picture of my life God had planned for me. I didn't understand that God had a mandate on my life, and all the people, places and things were preordained by God before I entered my mother's womb. Lord have mercy; there is no way I could have known that. This is phenomenal.

"Do not fear, nor be afraid; Have I not told you from that time and declared it" You are my witnesses, Is there a God besides Me? Indeed, there is no other Rock; I know not one."

Isaiah 44:8

"The Lord is my light and my salvation, Whom shall I fear. The Lord is the strength of my life; Of whom shall I be afraid?"

Psalm 27:1

Notes to Myself

2

Traumatized

It wasn't until a couple of years ago when the Lord laid it on my heart to return to the book and do this research. I believe this information is definitely needed for some of the readers that will eventually read this book. If you've ever been sabotaged or know someone who has been; or perhaps lost something that was very dear to you; I believe feelings and symptoms of being traumatized effects our well-being. However, so often we continue to move forward.

I now realize that I was actually traumatized after closing the business, but I was trying to move forward as if nothing happened. One such meaning of being traumatized is *"an event or situation that causes great distress and disruption."* I was in distress, and certainly living through a great disruption." My life had become a complete shamble of pain and confusion, unrest, and awkwardness. Have you ever felt like you could cut a hole in your skin and pull the pain out? Another such meaning for traumatized **is** *"Subject to lasting shock as a result of an emotionally disturbing experience or physical injury."* Through that traumatic state, I had no one to talk to, family or friends. Getting through was still a long and arduous process.

At some point, the devil often sat on my left shoulder and whispered *"commit suicide."* But, one day the Holy Spirit moved in on the enemies words so fast, before I had an instant to think about it. But, the Holy Spirit made me turn my focus elsewhere as I began to pray and recited this scripture:

"Casting all your care upon Him; for He cares for You." 1 Peter 5:7

To know this and apply it are two different things. Learning to really apply the word of God in your life is a process, and although it may take some time for any one new in the word, know that it can be done.

I read an article that stated "*Emotional and Psychological Trauma is the result of extraordinarily stressful events that shatter your sense of security, making you feel helpless and vulnerable in a dangerous world.*" The article also stated that, "*Traumatic experiences often involve a threat to life or safety, but any situation that leaves you feeling overwhelmed and alone can be traumatic, even if it doesn't involve physical harm. It's not the objective facts that determine whether an event is traumatic, but your subjective emotional experience of the event. The more frightened and helpless you feel, the more likely you are to be traumatized.*"

The article also stated some of the psychological and emotional symptoms of trauma I experienced while going through traumatic stress:

- ***Anger, irritability, mood swings***
- ***Guilt, shame, self-blame***
- ***Feeling sad and hopeless***
- ***Anxiety and fear***
- ***Withdrawing from others***
- ***Feeling disconnected or numb***

Below are the physical symptoms of trauma I experienced while going through this drastic change in my life:

- ***Insomnia and agitation***
- ***Fatigue***
- ***Difficulty concentrating***
- ***Edginess***

Until I began researching my experiences, I really did not know the depth of my past and what I was experiencing. Even though I was trying to move forward, I did not allow myself to fall prey to the situation. However, time continued to move on as life's issues materialized.

As always, there are going to be good times and bad times in your life; however, staying focused on what is necessary to survive is another issue. No one can walk in your shoes better than you can. No matter how hard they try or how many trials you endure, your shoes are made for walking only in your size. We can be sure that God truly has a plan that only you will be able to carry out. I truly had no idea what was in store for me as I began to walk this path of loneliness, with no peace, irritability and unrest. My mind became an endless ride on a fast moving roller coaster.

Recently, I've had an opportunity to speak with several people who have been sabotaged in their workplaces, and some of the experiences have been devastating. To think, that I had multiple things going on that was causing so much pain. I must have been an emotional wreck.

"*Life is a journey – a ride of endless means and emotions!*"

Mary V. Pate

Notes to Myself

3
The Awakening

When we awaken each morning, we probably do not think of the things that can transpire within our lives in a day. The thought never entered my mind, of the many chaotic things our lives can be entangled in during our lifespan. "I'm minding my own business, doing what I'm told, and still end up in a mess." How could this be? What did others see in me that I didn't know about myself? I was bewildered.

Let me awaken you to the beast in some workplaces. The beast called "sabotage." Now, this beast comes from another person's fear of something which causes them to react in such a way that it can ultimately destroy another person. *The Merriam-Webster's dictionary states "sabotage" as a deliberate damage done to property, installations, etc. e.g., by enemy agents or by hostile employees."* A *'Saboteur'* is a person who commits sabotage. In other words, saboteurs can cause you to lose your job, and very possibly, not get another one. Make no mistake about it; this person wants to destroy your life.

During these times, I became very vulnerable toward people, situations, and daily living. I found myself trying to trust people on some level, but it became increasingly more difficult for me to trust.

All over the country people are being fired from their jobs because of fear and sabotage. That says a lot for our country, employment, and stability in the workplace. The truth is there is no stability in the workplace. If pursued by law, a criminal suit against a company for "sabotage" can be very costly and difficult to prove, which is why so many people do not file complaints.

Thirty years ago many of us worked in corporate America and felt secure, complacent, and confident that our lives were complete because of a job, a pension, 401Ks, and other perks from our employer. You may have felt that everything is just fine in your life with all the benefits and amenities that came along with a great job. Currently, most of us have probably in some way been affected by downsizing, layoffs, and, yes, sabotage in the workplace. As of 2005, if you have been or are still in the same job for more than ten years, you need to "clap for Jesus." You've made a tenure that many will not make during these days and times.

If God has given you the gift of discernment, you know when something is lurking in the air, and you know whom the snakes are. If you don't know, ask God for more discernment, and to show you through revelations the things that are going on within your surroundings. There are always signs and more than one culprit. Dealing with snakes is another story. When God was redeeming Israel, and speaking to Jacob, He said, *"But now, thus says the Lord, who created you, O Jacob, And He who formed you, O Israel; " Fear not, for I have redeemed you; I have called you by your name; You are Mine. When you pass the waters, I will be with you; and through the rivers, they shall not overflow you. When you walk through the fire, you shall not be burned, Nor shall the flame scorch you."*

Isaiah 43:1-2

Now, I believe that when God said this, He meant whatever we are going through, as long as we trust Him, have faith in Him, He will never leave us nor forsake us. He didn't say it was going to be easy; he just took the burdens away, and said He will be with us. Dealing with Saboteurs, and going through the storms can be an awful trying time in your life, but hold on; God is still on the throne. During these times, I began to rely on God more and more. My trials and tribulations became more intense and strenuous on me.

The first time I actually evidenced any type of "sabotage," and there are a variety of ways this can be done, was via the company I was employed by before I started my agency. When they began the process of elimination, performance appraisals begin to come in from various areas. I received the information and realized certain employees appraisals were changed to either have them become downgraded or they would get laid off. Talk about "sabotage." Although I was not personally sabotaged in this case, others were. I remember feeling so bad about this, because I had actually met some of the employees being affected.

I believe this had such a devastating effect on me, more than I realized at the time. Often times we go through situations and circumstances that are unfamiliar to us; however, we must go through them. If God has it in the plan for your life, then essentially, you own it, although not recognizing the causes and effects it has, and will have on your life in the future. My journey in this particular area lasted a very long time.

As people, we probably don't think about the circumstances and situations we live through from time to time, but I have come to believe that everything we encounter has a purpose, whether we realize it at that moment or later in life.

For many years now, companies have terminated thousands of people, and I am sure it's not surprising to anyone today how some of these companies justify their reasons for laying off workers. Some cases have been from the recession, while many have been sabotaged.

"Life has a way of Knocking you down, and then lifts
You up to start the race again."

Mary V. Pate

Notes to Myself

4

Facing the Enemy

After closing my agency, I went south to live for a couple of years, and later returned to the northern states with my family. I was able to obtain employment through someone I considered at the time, to be a friend. And, although I only wanted a job, sometimes situations arise that you don't expect, but they come.

I was employed in the healthcare industry and reported directly to the president. I have to admit that during my many thoughts, I was hoping eventually I would be able to secure a position that would give me more management responsibilities, and hopefully longevity.

During the first three months, I was given rave reviews about my work. I was the greatest. Now, I began to think everything was going to be just fine. Approximately a month later, he engaged me in a conversation about my past life in the business world and as an entrepreneur. This was my first opportunity since working for him to really have a conversation with him on this level. I thought he would realize that I was a very knowledgeable person and this would give him an opportunity to pursue my strengths in his endeavors to further advance in the company, and the possibility of a more advanced position.

Unfortunately, my life became a living hell for the next three months. Now, you're probably saying to yourself, this man read her resume, interviewed her, screened and placed her in the job; a job that was very important to him. What could have possibly gone wrong? My first encounter with a "sabotage" process began.

Immediately, this man set me up to fail, and I felt daggers in my heart and the points twisting and slitting my every vessel. His attitude changed toward me; he became reclusive and subdued, short and negative in responses, absent from the office and not revealing how he could be reached. I knew I was in trouble, but continued through the struggle. Then, one day while retrieving documents from his office, he made an unbelievable statement and said: "you came here to steal my job, but that is not going to happen." First of all, I was shocked as I giggled a reply "I am so glad you realize I can do your job, and that is gratifying to know, but that is not my reason for being here." Now, his fear had come face to face with me. The snake had stuck out his ugly tongue and lashed at me. His insecure mannerism, and bulging eyes were glaring at me with hatred. This is a time to call on the name that is above all names, Jesus. Although it's difficult when you're standing in truth and facing the enemy; don't show fear, if you can help it. Control your emotions, and let God be God. I must admit controlling my emotions was difficult for me in several instances, because as far as I'm concerned it's a terrible feeling when someone is lying on you, and you're trying to do the best job you can for them.

Thereafter, he made it impossible for me to do an efficient job. With all the detailed responsibilities I had, he set me up for the kill. The responsibilities of the job depended a lot on his input; so his disappearing acts affected the outcome and end results of my job. My sixth month review had statements that seemed as if I did not know my head from a hole in the ground. Has anyone ever been there except me? Hello, I was in a den of lions, and they were waiting to have me for breakfast, lunch, dinner and a snack. The enemy was chewing on me, while my life unfolded in front of me. I had no one to help me, no one to talk to, But God. I felt like a mixed pan of hot greens sweltering in a boiling pot of water, dissolving to a place of nothingness. I wanted to scream. O' God, why was this happening to me? My answers were many light years away.

I was eventually told that he wanted a friend of his to have the job I was in; therefore, he needed to get rid of me.

I will introduce you to some of the "unclean spirits" we carry as people. Unclean spirits are embedded in our hearts, and will come forth from the ways we live our lives, some from generational struggles, and some from pure evilness that come forth at times.

In this particular case, some of the unclean spirits I encountered were from the Spirit of Haughtiness: prideful, egotistical, entitlement, self- assertion and a Lying Spirit: deceit, manipulation. Mankind walks in these spirits and so many more.

"As Your Life Unfolds from layers of the old, You begin to fade."

Mary V. Pate

Notes to Myself

5

Emotional Pain

Whenever we're traumatized, we now have emotional pain. Emotional pain comes from such things as hurt feelings, irritability, and hurtful issues in our past or present. I was encountering emotional wounds of fear, shame, abandonment, and rejection. I was an emotional mess. Although I was moving quickly, when I settled in for the night, I often had restless sleep. I was easily frustrated and often lashed out. I felt as if no one loved me, and the emotional feelings of abandonment were very prevalent during those times. But, the word says, *"Casting all your care, upon Him; for He careth for you."*

1 Peter 5:7

God cares for us and He wants us to release all our burdens upon Him. He knew that we would have problems and encounter situations during our lives that would be difficult for us to handle. Whenever we are going through emotional pain, and do not follow the word of God, we allow our emotional problems to escalate, making ourselves available to spirits of anger, hatred, bitterness, rejection and abandonment. These spirits lie dormant and continually remind us of why we are drenching in pain, and why we are so angry.

Although it's easy to say now, we must cast these burdens over to God to be released from all the pain and unforgiveness. We must forgive ourselves to understand the importance of forgiving others. When God is in the mix of what is going on in our lives, we might find that emotional healing may take a very long time. He must heal you of all the mess that you have ever endured throughout your lifetime. Therefore, He is taking away small pieces of your pain little by little. Everything with God is a process. He does not move from A- to -Z quickly, but in baby steps instead that will heal every fiber of your being. Lord have mercy, this can take a long time. You must remember that there may have been hurts that are unresolved, and hiding in your subconscious mind for years, and all of a sudden, the time comes to uproot all the struggles and forgotten issues. The roots of those issues have now been birthed and invading your life. Cry out to God, and hold onto His unchanging hand.

It is imperative that you identify the emotional wounds that are holding you back from releasing yourself of the pain. Here are a few symptoms of someone who has emotional wounds:

Irritability: *becoming irritable or frustrated with another person, although that person may have done nothing wrong.*

Sensitivity: *this could be about an event from your past: Many times we are carrying issues from our past that we believe are over and forgotten; however, the mere mention of that event makes us irritable or upset.*

Unforgiveness: *not releasing a person from your mind or heart who has hurt you in the past.*

Anger: *this can easily show up in outbursts when you are hurt and a wound has been lingering for a very long time.*

These are just a few areas that cause us to have emotional pain, but you must realize that God loves you very much; and He wants you to be whole in all areas of your life. In my case, I began to feel embarrassed, and ashamed. I felt as though I had failed when I closed the business. Then, feelings of loneliness, and brokenness set in, and there was no one to make me feel better. I believe at this low point, God picked me up to keep me alive, because had it not been for Him, I know I wouldn't be here today. When we are going through this pain, we don't think about Jesus, who bore our grief, pain, sorrows and affliction; and He did it all for us. We don't say to ourselves, "He's already taken care of this for me, so why am I allowing this emotional pain to infiltrate my life?"

"Surely He has borne our griefs, And carried our sorrows; Yet we esteemed Him stricken, Smitten by God, and afflicted. But He was wounded for our transgressions, He was bruised for our iniquities; The chastisement for our peace was upon Him, And by His stripes we are healed."

Isaiah 53:4-5

During these seasons of pain, we need to focus on what God has done for us to deliver us from the burdens we are carrying even though we are in a painful state of mind. OK, we are all human, and want the best for ourselves, as well as our love ones. I can tell you that fear may play a very important part of your life; however, when you realize that you didn't die from whatever you are faced with, then you realize that you have to muster up some "faith" to keep moving forward.

"And God will wipe away every tear from your eyes; there shall be no more death, nor sorrow, nor crying. There shall be no more pain, for the former things have passed away."

Jeremiah 21:4

Notes to Myself

6

Intimidation

I have often been around people who are intimidated by me or someone else. It's really a very sad sight to see. Sometimes, these people will not look you directly in the eye. You can feel their insecurities gushing through their veins. It's almost like they hate you but don't want anyone to know it. As sad as this can be, many people walk in the spirit of intimidation. You can never do anything right as far as they're concerned, and they don't feel secure in connecting with you directly. Personally, I have had many encounters with these types of people, and quite frankly, they become a pure nuisance. From some of my past encounters; I've often wanted to tell them, "just get a life, build your self-confidence, getting right with God is a great start." It's actually a very tiring situation to have daily encounters with these types of people. They usually have some type of drama going on, and always need to have control of everything. If these people only had this type of self control over the spirit of intimidation that is operating in their lives, what a wonderful day it would be for everyone.

Intimidation implies that a person has a fear or an inferiority complex toward another person. At times they will try to make you feel less of a person than you really are. This is because the intimidated person must feel superior over you. Intimidated people hate it when you do something good that commands attention from others or is worthwhile. Don't sit back and wait for them to give you any congratulations about anything you've done. You will probably be waiting a very long time. A spirit of haughtiness is controlling that person.

I often encountered these kinds of spirits, and it's very awkward to try and communicate with them on a daily basis, but one thing I do know is that no matter how comfortable you try to make them feel, nothing works. It's really very simple; nothing works because intimidation is a heart issue. All heart issues must be changed through God, not ourselves. It's not very often that you will find one person admitting to another that they are intimidated by the other, if at all.

Sabotage is an ugly, un-forgetful event that no one should have to encounter. However, I believe it happens more often than we realize or perhaps some people don't tell. Unfortunately, sabotage usually stems from pride, arrogance, control and fear by one of the people who are setting up the demise of another. We cannot forget another very important factor. In the workplace, intimidation also stems from a person walking in fear of losing their position, such as a manager fearing that one of their subordinates or colleagues is after their job or one they may be seeking.

Unfortunately, many intimidated people, don't realize that feelings of self-worth has nothing to do with the person they are fearful of; but their own lack of self-confidence. The worst thing is that they cause havoc in your life and others, so you can imagine how they feel about themselves. So many times, these people act out, and lie on you and to you in hopes of getting rid of you. I had the unpleasant experience to work with many people who walked in the spirit of intimidation. It's one thing when you work with one person, but when there are many; it's a nightmare. There is a non-stop, constant, up-in–your-face-mess.... It's always something, and you don't have to do anything but enter the room. These people can very easily cause you to have a very bad day at work.

Intimidation is a "fruit" that is listed under the stronghold Spirit of Fear. This plays a very big part in the lives of so many people today. Things have drastically changed in the workplace, and because of the lack of work, people are jockeying for position, and they don't care who they run over, kill, beat down, lie about, or steal to get what they want. In other words, there is no respect for one another; there is no love in this area, and people will do whatever is necessary to get what you have, while pleading in the name of Jesus. There are so many lost souls in this world, and the faces of America in the workplace has changed in suits, and dresses that say, "I want what you have, and I am going to take it by force."

The Stronghold Spirit of Jealousy has such "fruits" listed as revenge, spite, hate, cruelty, and obsession. There are others; however, this list should give you more understanding of how unclean spirits, or strongholds can and will manifest in our lives without giving you any notice.

Genesis 37, Joseph's brothers wanted to kill him because of Jealousy. Their father favored Joseph and gave him a tunic of many colors, and the brothers were jealous. Jealousy is a dangerous, unclean spirit. This spirit will smile in your face while slashing your throat.

"So it came to pass when Joseph had come to his brothers that they stripped Joseph of his tunic, the tunic of many colors that was on him. They then took him and cast him into a pit. And the pit was empty, there was no water in it."

Genesis 37:23-24

Although other circumstances and situations were written in these scriptures, this is a perfect example of how deadly the "spirit of jealousy" can be. Imagine being thrown into a pit with no water; you would actually hit rock bottom.

Notes to Myself

7

The Spirit Of Fear

When I think of the torment one must go through when they fear someone or something, I would have to say it's like fighting a bear in the woods, and it's just you and him. Fear is a tormenting spirit that first affects your mind, and then your spirit. Ah, the spirit of fear opens a passageway for the devil to have free reign in your life. This reminds me of the time when Israel was assured of God's help in *Isaiah 41:10*, "*Fear not for I am with you. I will strengthen you, I will keep you.*"

Fear of being hurt will keep us out of relationships and intimacy. But, *1 John 4:18* says, "*There is no fear in love, but perfect love casts out fear, because fear involves torment. But he who fears has not been made perfect in love.*" I am sure we all know at least one person who lives in this kind of fear. I believe they're living in frustration, a life of torment and hell. Fear of loving, that just nudged my spirit as I was reading this over. No matter what has happened in our lives, *"the fear of loving"* must be a serious life killer. In opposition to that God's love is so wonderful like the feel of silk. His love comforts and counsels us. He wraps His arms around you and makes everything alright. It's a love that you can count on when there is no other. His love makes you feel safe, secure, and gives you that peace you need when all else is lost. If we leave it up to the enemy, we would be walking in fear all the time.

Fear hinders you from reaching your potential and the anointed call God has on your life. Fear comes along to steal all your joy; I call this a "life killer." But Jesus said in, *John 14:28 "Peace I leave with you. My peace I give to you."* Here's a phrase I always repeat to myself "I am responsible for making me fear proof, because I walk by faith and not by sight." I was watching one of Dr. Creflo Dollars' programs, and he stated, "Fear is believing what the devil says; Faith is believing what God says." I agree.

Fear comes to contradict what faith is saying. Fear is the opposite of faith. Fear's job is to stop you from doing what the Lord says. Fear's job is to stop you from reaching your God-given destiny. Fear's job is to break you down. Fear's job is to steal your joy. Fear's job is to remove your name out of the Lamb's book. Fear is the devil's work. As long as there's fear in your life, God's will for your life can not go forth, because you're standing in your own way. Squash the neck of fear, like Jesus did to the snake in the Garden of Gethsemane.

Build your confidence and self-esteem. Encourage yourself to go after what God has for you. When you are going through storms, this process seems so far beyond your comprehension, but that is the time to build your courage and move forward. I can't stress this enough that your faith Walk is your birth right from God. So give it your all, and allow God to do a good work in you. It may seem a little strange to others, but remember God views everything from a spiritual perspective. And as a people, we should begin to view things spiritually as well. Remember the scripture that speaks about "His thoughts and His ways being higher than ours?" Well, they are higher than ours, because God looks at everything about us from another dimension. The answer to this problem and getting a little closer to God is that we must stop thinking along the same lines as we always have. Increase in your knowledge of Him and find out how Kingdom living is really executed.

"For My thoughts are not your thoughts, neither are your ways My ways, says the Lord. For as the heavens are higher than the earth, so are My ways higher than your ways and My thoughts than your thoughts."

Isaiah 55:8-9

I remember the revelation I received from this scripture, and I thought to myself although I am five-one inches in height, I have to see God, I have to hear God, and I have to think like God, or at least somewhere over and above where I stand to recognize that His way of doing anything will never succumb to my level. Actually, I had to bring my thoughts up so much higher and expect that whatever His plans are, He will do everything beyond what I can obtain for myself. Therefore, I had to learn to step back, and see what God would do in any circumstance or situation in my life, and grab hold of what He has to offer me.

Good, bad, or indifferent, my thoughts and ways would never add up to the outcome He has for any circumstance or situation in my life. Let's be clear, the Father did not say that life was always going to be peaches and cream with a cherry on top; however, He did say that if we allow Him to orchestrate our lives, no matter the effect on us at that moment, everything will eventually work out in our favor. The worst thing you will have to deal with is always seeing yourself on the losing end; however, in retrospect, in everything God allows you to go through, there are lessons to be learned. Your best days are yet to come.

Under the Spirit of Fear are many "fruits" that materialize. You may recognize them if for any reason you have walked in a spirit of fear.

a) Procrastination: to put a task off, postpone, or delay needlessly.

b) Torment: to worry or annoy excessively; torture, pain

c) Nightmares: a dream arousing feelings of intense fear, horror, and distress.

d) Apprehension: fearful or uneasy anticipation of the future; dread

e) Phobias: a feeling of agitation and anxiety caused by the presence or imminence of danger.

f) Nervousness: easily agitated or distressed; high-strung or jumpy.

g) Becoming overwhelmed: to affect deeply in mind or emotion

If you are experiencing any of the above feelings, and there are others, you are now walking in the "**stronghold Spirit of Fear** and its fruits. The fruit are what I call the "offspring of those nasty little strongholds" so many people are walking in, and do not understand how they can live free of the unclean spirits that the bible states we do not have to live in. Actually, so many people, church folks, who believe they can and will walk around with these unclean spirits for the balance of their lives. As time went on, I was able to understand, and disarm stronghold spirits and their fruit.

"For God did not give us a spirit of timidity (of cowardice, of craven and cringing and fawning fear), but (He has given us a spirit) of power and love and of calm and well-balanced mind and discipline and self-control.

2 Timothy 1:7

Notes to Myself

8

Moving in Faith

Although I had done this so many times in my life, it was so different when the time came to step out on faith for God. I realized it was the first time I was commissioned to do something that I could not see. But I knew that eventually I had to step out and be obedient to God.

"By faith we understand that the worlds were framed by the word of God, so that the things which are seen were not made of things which are visible." Hebrew 11:3

The things that are seen is the universe, and the things that are visible is God. The evidence of things not seen are those blind areas that are still in the spirit realm, but you can't see or touch them yet. Some may say that you have to take a chance on moving through some challenges, and opportunities, yet you don't know the outcome. But this you do know, God is faithful, and He rewards those who diligently seek Him.

In my past, God has given me the "Go" signal to travel places and do things for Him, and what I thought was going to happen really didn't manifest, but another move of God showed up. You see, when the Holy Spirit is maturing and training you, sometimes He may commission you to do a particular job (it's usually something that He knows you can do very well), but the assignment is a gift that He is bringing forth through you. You may or may not have known the gift existed or perhaps never used it before, but now is the time for God to show you something special He has given you. Sons and daughters of God, I can assure you that it is just another awesome move of God while He is taking you on your faith walk. Usually, when that happens, God changed that situation into another opportunity for Him to manifest Himself, and so that you can see His glory. The one thing you must know is that opportune assignment was to see your faithfulness toward Him. Whatever happened was for your benefit at that moment and the glory of God, because He showed up. Amen.

What is God looking for in us when He says, "Step out on faith?" Stepping out on faith for God is grabbing hold of your feelings and emotions, letting go of all the fear, moving out, and pressing toward the goal.

He wants you to use the authority and the power that He speaks of: *"Behold I give you the authority to trample on serpents and scorpions, and over all the power of the enemy, and nothing shall by any means hurt you." Luke 10:19.* He wants you to use your boldness and confidence. These things are already in you. All you need to do is begin to walk it out in faith.

"Therefore, do not cast away your confidence, which has great reward. For you have need of endurance, so that after you have done the will of God, you may receive the promise."

Hebrew 10:35-36

The faith walk says," I am no longer standing still." The Faith Walk says, "I am going to do something, but I will stay in the will of God." You must be able to walk in the spirit, in God's will, and in God's way. Know that even when we slip we are only human. God will be right there to get us back on track. God's got this! Hallelujah! But before we go out on our faith walk, we must believe and trust in God and diligently seek Him.

"But without Faith it is impossible to please Him, for He who comes to God must believe that He is, and that He is a rewarder of those who diligently seek Him."

Hebrew 11:6

There are several types of gifts of faith. Natural faith is common human faith that everyone has. Saving faith comes when someone receives Christ and believes in the sacrifice of Jesus Christ. A measure of faith is the faith that God gives every believer to grow into. The measure of faith helps the believer grow and operate in his/her spiritual gifts. The gift of faith comes from the Holy Spirit for the purpose of manifesting a certain activity of the Holy Spirit thru the believer, such as signs and wonders.

The faith I am speaking of here is the supernatural manifestation of the Holy Spirit. You will find these scriptures regarding the spiritual gifts of faith in 1 Corinthians 12:4-11.

The power gifts of faith is the result of being filled with the Holy Spirit. This supernatural manifestation of faith is a gift of the Holy Spirit that He will use through you for a special occasion or time, which enables you to believe in, or to expect, an extraordinary demonstration of the power of God. It is a belief that you trust and believe in God so much that he will manifest Himself through this action on your behalf. So remember, it is the Holy Spirit who will move on your behalf, because there is no way you can accomplish this goal yourself. You must have a certain amount of faith for this supernatural manifestation of faith, which is unexplainable, to occur for you and the receiver. This supernatural manifestation of the Holy Spirit moves suddenly, and as He wills. It is instant and passing; meaning, this faith is when the Holy Spirit moves on your behalf instantly and continues to flow through you and outward.

It literally feels like the Holy Spirit says, "Bam, it's done. Now let's move onto the next thing at hand." I believe this determines how strong your belief is in the Holy Spirit, and that He will move on your behalf; there are no limits we need to put on God. Supernatural manifestations of faith are actually seeing the Glory of God being manifested before your eyes.

Oh, what an awesome God we serve. Just to think that His power, His might moves because you're favored by Him, loved by Him, and you're walking in His will and His way for His glory. Lord have mercy, this is great stuff.

For whatever is born of God is victorious over the world; and this is the victory that conquers the world, even our faith.

1 John 5:4

Notes to Myself

9

Jezebel Spirit

As I continued on toward upward mobility, or so I thought, I found myself in another messy situation. I was enjoying the steady flow of getting a pay check; only to find out later that I was being set up again. I began to think this could not be happening. What is going on? Why was I constantly going through this? Was there something in the water I was drinking? Did I look like a woman from Mars? No, this time I was in a position where I was the first African American woman in this particular job. My mere presence upset some of them, to say nothing of the fact that I actually did my job better than my predecessors, or so I was told. And so, the saga began.

For one year, I was employed at a healthcare facility as a marketing representative and was able to completely fill all the beds in the home. If you have any understanding of this type of business; the main goal is to fill every bed in the facility with residents coming from hospitals. That is how the facility earned its income. Being confident in myself, I filled the facility to its capacity; such was never done by my predecessors. After completely filling all the beds in the facility, my colleagues would have preferred the rooms were empty than for me to get recognition of success or achievability. I realized this because at times the lead manager would try to hold back from taking patients, until I went to our administrator about the situation, then things changed and patients were allowed in.

After a year, I went to a second facility, and I had to work with another employee, supposedly as a team member. My team member was a jezebel spirit that had the management personnel rapped around her fingers. A typical example of jezebel is being a controlling spirits. Later, there was a sabotage plan set up against me by my colleague and the managers. As before, spirits of prejudice and racism was very prevalent at this location as well. The person who hired me for the position left for another job before I got to the location, so I was not received very nicely.

The devil is always busy. The facility was eventually sold to another company and they opted not to hire the administrator, so she tried everything she could to get rid of me before leaving the company. The administrator was also a very good friend of my colleague, which did not help my case. When she couldn't get rid of me, a write-up was left against me for the new managers coming in that was completely against every fiber of my being. Get this, I was asked to sign the write-up. People of God, you don't have to sign anything that you are not in agreement with. Obviously, she must have thought I was a very stupid woman.

When the hand of the enemy is alive and kicking, you can believe there is always more than one person involved. As some will say, "jezebel and her followers." Some people will do anything to destroy another to keep their job. Remember, no one is going to be on your side against their boss. The truth is there were actually six people that I know of who were involved in this plot. However, it doesn't matter how many persons are really infiltrated in these type of situations, because, eventually they get the entire staff to be on their side. In instances like this, we have to remember "vengeance is mine, says the Lord."

Remember folks, what God has for you is for you. Although it may take a long time to get there, do not give up. I am like an ever-ready battery; I just keep on ticking. God will never give up on us, so we should never give up on Him. Press through the anger, frustration, torment, fears, hurt, and the pain; God is at hand. Do not sell your soul to the devil.

Consider the work of God; for who can make straight what He has made crooked? In the day of prosperity be joyful, But in the day of adversity consider; Surely God has appointed the one as well as the other, so that man can find out nothing that will come after him."

Ecclesiastes 7:13-14

In other words, God is the one that allows adversity to come upon us. Although adversity does not feel good, God allows these things to happen because He wants to get your attention, your obedience, and your faith in Him. In the future, He will use you in a mighty way in the Kingdom. God is also teaching you how to become humble. I believe when these kind of things are happening in your life, no one can help you. There are some things you must go through to understand where God is taking you. This is not to say that you will not encounter many people along the way that believe they are your saviors. Nothing is farther from the truth than mankind saving you when God is working out His will through you.

Well, I looked at the same scenario for myself. God had allowed the wiles of the devil to trap me in my finances and employment because it was for His glory when and how I was going to be delivered out of the hands of the enemy, not my own. Remember, there is a reason and a season for everything, nothing just happens. Being in debt is of an evil spirit, but God is able.

"But if I cast out demons in the Spirit of God, surely the kingdom of God has come upon you. Or how can one enter a strong man's house and plunder his goods, unless he first binds the strong man. And then he will plunder his house."

Matthew 12:28-29

So you see God allowed the evil spirit to enter my house, my life, as He did with **Job**. God set this up from the onset to bring me into His glorious way of doing things, and to advance His kingdom. Trust me, there were many years of pain and teachings by the Holy Spirit as He led me into my life of today. During the time when I was going through the wilderness, I did not have revelation knowledge of the word of God, and so I did not know how to fight the good fight. It took me some time, but I learned. The key is for you to be teachable. So, the Holy Spirit had me under His wings, while He allowed the demons to bind me up and plundered my house. I often screamed "*Help me Lord, but help did not come.*" God had a plan that I knew absolutely, unequivocally nothing about. How could I have known anything except that I was sinking fast?

"*I will instruct you and teach you in the way you should go; I will counsel you and watch over you.*"

Psalm 32:8

God wants to teach us how to live the life He has preordained for us. You may not realize it, but the Holy Spirit can teach you everything you need to know about your walk with the Lord. When I say "everything" I mean "everything." It took years and many trials and tribulations for me to acknowledge this, but now I say, "*For I neither received it from man, nor was I taught it, but it came through the revelation of Jesus Christ.*"

Galatians 1:12

Meanwhile, back at my place of employment, my enemies were very busy. There were so many lies being told against me as the wars increased. The management had now told my colleagues, and some of them stopped talking to me. The ultimate goal was to get me out of the job I had and fill it with someone of a different race, as was the colleague I shared responsibilities with. Imagine being up against these type of prejudices and issues every day. The response to my getting fired was that the hospital staff was not happy with my lack of success in getting residents into the facility. However, I did not have full authority to allow residents to come into the facility without the approval of my leadership, and at times, she did not allow that, or would purposely slow the process although she knew the repercussions. Therefore, my hands were tied, and in that business, slow decisions gave your competition more time to take your place. This was the method of sabotage that was used against me in this case. So, my boss set me up to fail.

I was in serious distress, and must have been operating through my outer body in a way that was unsettling to me. I was so scared of what my life was turning into, and I felt so bad from all the lies and gossip that was being told throughout the facility about me, but there was nothing I could do.

Now that I have grown in Christ and know the call on my life, I can still see the faces of people I worked with and discern how they viewed me before I was fired. Again, everyone I talked to was against me, and no one would talk with me. Isolation for me at that time was very difficult, but not anymore. Before being told to pack my things and leave the facility, I must have been in a zombie state of mind. Certainly, I had feelings of abuse, neglect, abandonment, rejection, not being accepted, and thrown away. God was allowing me to go through all that pain, and for what reason. I asked Him, what had I done in the past that He would allow me to go through all that? I had asked for forgiveness and repented for all my sins a few years prior; so I asked again, and yet I was still suffering. No one is going to walk with you when you're getting fired. I must have felt like Jesus did when all the disciples left Him in the Garden of Gethsemane.

At the time, I did not think of the **Job** story; nor, that God allows adversity in our lives as well. I was just lost and in so much pain; and worst yet, I had no one to talk to about it. I didn't have the answers; I was ashamed, and I was embarrassed. I don't know if any of you have ever been in a situation where people will act as though they are your friends, but drilling daggers through your heart while looking at you in your face. These are the kinds of situations I encountered daily by my leadership before I was fired. The woman that hired me at this facility returned and treated me so nice in front of everyone there; then requested to speak to me privately and became an entirely different animal once the door was closed. She talked down to me, belittled me, and chastised me about being there. Needless to say, I was shocked.

Lord have mercy; I didn't know about "unclean spirits" at that time. But, I was surrounded by witches, and they all hated me.

My team member was very sneaky, and would often come into the office, smile, speak to me like she was my best friend, and walk out of the door and go to our supervisor's office and lie on me. Many times, she didn't call into the office with her whereabouts, and our leader would always ask me where she was. Of course, my answer was always "I haven't heard from her," and the manager acted as though she was upset with me. But, no matter what happened, the leadership always accepted her disappearing acts, and whatever she told them became gospel. I often thought to myself, "What is That?" "Why do they always believe her lies?" I later learned that many of the things she told them were lies that I had indeed heard from her, that she was trying to place people into the facility, and I would not allow them to come in. This was part of the conspiracy against me to have me fired. This person was always in control of everything and everyone. I later learned that she didn't call into the office to speak to me; however, she was calling and speaking to the manager, as the plot thickened against me.

Although I didn't know it at the time, I was encountering "jezebel spirits." This spirit took control of the situation to get rid of me, to tear me down, belittling me, having control and manipulation of the office and getting away with it. One asset jezebel's have is the ability to control and manipulate their surroundings, as long as they can possibly get away with it. And, jezebel spirits are very good at getting people to follow them and have the followers do the unclean spirits' dirty work, particularly the leaders.

If you read about the church in Thyatira in Revelations and Jezebel in 1 Kings, you will see the many things Jezebel did to others and the killing of the prophets to gain control of everything she wanted. The influence or spirit of Jezebel leads the professed people and leaders of God into spiritual idolatry.

1 Kings 21:11-15 "So the men of his city, the elders and nobles who were inhabitants of the city, did as Jezebel had sent to them, as it was written in the letters which she had sent to them. They proclaimed a Fast, and seated Naboth with high honor among the people. And two men, scoundrels, lied *on Naboth in the presence of the people, saying", Naboth has blasphemed God and the King!" Then they sent to Jezebel saying, "Naboth has been stoned and is dead." And it came to pass, when Jezebel heard that Naboth had been stoned and was dead, that Jezebel said to Ahab, "Arise, take possession of the vineyard of Naboth the Jezreelite, which he refused to give you for money for Naboth is not alive, but dead."*

Ahab went down and took possession of the vineyard. This was the same type of spirit (s) I was confronting every day, spirits that had the control of leadership in the companies I worked for; and I know now that perhaps those spirits could see that I would be immovable if they had to deal with me by themselves. The spirit of jezebel destroys to achieve unlawful gain. It is a spirit of false accusations and deceit in order to destroy the influence or the life of the innocent to gain control of everything and everyone around them.

Although we often refer to jezebel's as women, they are men as well. Later on, I encountered these spirits through men. Jezebels usually appear to leaders', and they will then use their influence to dominate and control others use the Leaders power as the forefront while they manipulate and control situations in a very cunning way. In *1 Kings 21:8* it states, *"And she wrote letters in Ahab's name, sealed them with his seal, and sent the letters to the elders and the nobles who were dwelling in the city with Naboth."* Here again, Jezebel used her manipulation and control via the leader, while remaining in the background and getting what she wanted.

My heart is always in the right place to help whenever there is anything I can do to get meaningful results out of a bad situation. I am a results -oriented person. At that time, we were not getting clients into the facility as we should, and I had not heard from my team member, who was supposed to call me every day with a client list. I decided to ask one of the supervisor's to go with me to the hospital; I would then introduce her to the staff we normally did business with, in hopes that they would feel better about our facility and send us clients. I followed through and made my administrator knowledgeable of my plans, and we went to the hospital. Obviously it was a good gesture and I knew it normally would have worked; however, now I was working against their plan of action against me. The plot thickened when we returned. I was chastised, and criticized like you wouldn't believe, and the administrator acted as though I didn't inform him that I was going to the hospital. Unfortunately, when I began to get stoned, the supervisor that went with me didn't stand with me. I went to her office and asked her to come with me and verify the process we had gone through, and she would not help me. They knew I had done a good deed, they were not expecting that, and so, they speeded up the process to get rid of me.

The excuse for my demise at that job was that I was causing our partners to refuse to send clients to the facility by not responding to them in a timely manner. However; the manager, my immediate supervisor, the business contacts and my colleague were all in on getting me fired. Even if my colleague had called with potential clients, I could not allow anyone into the facility without the permission of my supervisor; they all knew that, and used it against me.

Jezebels hate spiritual authority. In Hebrews, Jezebel means "without cohabitation." They can't live or work with those that will not be dominated by them, or equal to. Therefore, everyone that stands in their way must go. It's all about control for Jezebels, and whenever they confront you in a submissive way, believe me, they have a thought out plan for your demise. Jezebel spirits do not like competition; however, as her colleague, I was working inside, and she was supposed to be working on the outside.

To make things worse after being terminated from the position, the manager that I reported to who usually gave her approval for a patient to come into the facility called me at home the night I got fired and said, "you can't file a law suit because I've already checked that information." Can a person get any meaner than that? Through lies, deception, and just pure meanness, some people will crucify you, take you down off the cross, put you in the grave, and pour dirt on your face......My Lord, help me Jesus! I also spoke with the supervisor who went with me to the hospital, and asked her why didn't she come to the office and support me. She only said "I am sorry, but I couldn't."

1 Samuel 15:23 tells us, "Rebellion is as the sin of witchcraft, and stubbornness is as iniquity and idolatry."

The Jezebel spirit is one of rebellion against God and His Word, and commits sinful acts of witchcraft. I've encountered several Jezebel's since the beginning of all my problems here, and identifying them is much easier now. The Holy Spirit is so awesome, as He teaches you everything He needs you to know for the ministry you are going to embark upon. Painful as it may be, it's always to benefit others, and to Glorify God.

My God, I give you the glory for opening my eyes, for saving me, and for loving me, through all my lack of knowledge. But, now I see.

Now, here are the unclean spirits I encountered everyday while in this position.

Stronghold Spirits of Lying:

a) Lies
b) Deceit
c) Manipulation
d) Hypocrisy
e) Exaggerations

Stronghold Spirits of Haughtiness:

a) Controlling spirit
b) Entitlement
c) Arrogance
d) Racism
e) Pride
f) Ambition

Stronghold Spirit of Perversion:

a) Rebellion
b) Homosexuality
c) Seducing spirit

This will help you understand some of the unclean spirits you may encounter each day in your workplace. Begin to recognize them on the people you are dealing with on a daily basis; you will be amazed once you learn this information, if you are not familiar with it already. Also, the strongholds are the "lid spirits" (like a top on a jar) while the "fruit of the spirit" are underneath or inside of the jar. I hope this will give you more understanding of the strongholds and their fruits.

"Wherefore by their fruits ye shall know them."

Matthew 7:20

Notes to Myself

10

Spider Web Entanglement

This period of my life was so awkward and disturbing for me. Nothing seemed to work, no matter how I tried. I truly did not understand why I was traveling on a downward spiral in my life. I asked God to help, I believed His word, I trusted Him, yet nothing seemed to change.

I then found employment in the construction industry. The first day I entered the workplace, it was like a story out of a suspense novel. I later realized I was in a den of witches. The leadership was arrogant, they spoke filthy curse words in the workplace, and they had some of the worst personalities I had encountered. They didn't give me an opportunity to learn my daily responsibilities before they complained about my work and gossiped to others. This place was worse than the last. I couldn't believe it. I was a miserable sister, and still couldn't understand why God would allow me to go through this. Coming from a corporate background, and then as an entrepreneur, these types of actions were appalling to say the least.

This was also the first time I encountered someone who actually told me they wanted my job. When this happened, I could not believe what I was hearing. I simply said to the person "You were here before I came; I don't understand why you didn't get the job before I arrived." Silence was my answer. Throughout the years, there would be several more times someone told me they wanted my job.

Within three months of working at the facility, there was talk of a customer's missing $10,000 check. I didn't pay much attention to the talk because I had not seen it, nor did I have the check. However, at the end of my trial period of three months, I needed to take a day off or I would have died at that place. I just needed a break from my surroundings, so I took a long weekend. It was at that time when the plot was thickening.

These people were terrible; they would stand directly in front of my desk and talk about me as if I weren't there. I would clean up particular aspects of my job, and they would blatantly give the credit to others. I was desperate. I often asked God, "Why were they treating me so meanly, and speaking about me as if I'm not there?" Has this ever happened to anyone except me? I now know that was a part of the processing God was taking me through, humbling me. God was teaching me that although I was going through hell, I would eventually be humbled to a level that I was not ready to conceive at that particular time. However, in time, those types of situations would be like butter melting in a hot pot.

Being treated that way made me recall my high school years, when some of the female students would walk past me and call me every name except a "child of God," and definitely not my correct name. I later learned it was because I was of a light complexion. I didn't understand at the time, but later I was informed that some African Americans don't favor some of us that have light complexions particularly when they are of dark complexions. It's so sad, because none of us are more privileged whether dark-or light-skinned in this race in America. For your information, if you are ever in this type of situation in your workplace, and are receiving harassment from a supervisor, please visit the website for the US Equal Employment Opportunity Commission. There are laws against this type of harassment, and it is no longer tolerated.

On my day off, one woman sat at my desk and did my work. This was the same woman who actually told me she wanted my job! I returned the next day, and as I entered the office, I was immediately called in to the manager's office. To my shock, I was confronting the head honcho, his supervisor and the lead administrative person. Ironically, the lead administrative person was crying. She stated that they had found the $10,000 check behind a tray on my desk. I knew that was a lie; however, I couldn't prove it, so I was definitely being sabotaged again. I almost felt sorry for her as she told me about the check, then I thought that she deserved it, for all the hell she caused me. I had two other persons that put work on my desk daily. One of them was the woman who stated she wanted my job, and sat at my desk the day I was out. You don't have to be a rocket scientist to figure that one out.

Remember, the devil is always on his job. He will have you do ungodly acts, and then make you look like a fool while humiliating you. My coworker was being used by her leadership in a way that caused her a lot of pain because she knew they used her to play out their lie against me. Shame on them, my position ended there.

Have you seen the movie "*Philadelphia* with Tom Hanks?" He played Mr. Bennett who was set up by his coworkers to make it seem as though he was not executing his work assignments as a lawyer. However, it was not his work habits that he was sabotaged for, but his coworkers' fear of his disease, Aids. These people were walking in fear of something that they did not understand.

"Behold the Lord's hand is not shortened that it cannot save; neither His ear heavy that it cannot hear."

Isaiah 59:1

I read an article recently about the spider's web of entanglement and how he thinks he can entrap and destroy. If any of you have gone through or have experienced false accusations, sabotage, conspiracies in your workplace, you definitely understand the plight of the spider web entanglement. The devil's children are at work, doing their job, while our Father in Heaven is allowing them to do what needs to be done for you. This could be much worse for some of you if you don't stand on the word of God, or not in a true place to believe that God has your back. Nothing just happens.

I must remind you that all these adversities made me get closer to God; although many times I still felt like **Job.** God allowed the devil to attack **Job** in many ways. **Job** was a very wealthy man, yet he lost everything, sickness and disease came against his body, but He never lost faith in God. That is the key; although you may go through hell during your life time, remaining close to God is the key.

I've taken this information from the New King James version study bible, in the Book of Job, and it states: ***At one time*** *or another almost everyone has felt like Job. While going through trials and times of suffering, we are often over whelmed by self- pity. We want an explanation for why God allows trials to happen to us. The Book of Job records the troubling questions, the terrifying doubts, and the real anguish of a sufferer. The Book of Job can help us in the time when we are surrounded with troubles by giving us a glimpse of God's perspective on our suffering. Just like Job, we must learn to submit to the Almighty God and accept by faith that He has a good plan for us.*

I was determined to find my purpose, "Why was I born into this world?" I wanted to know why I was going through so many hurdles, ups and downs. I knew I wasn't born to be poor and to live in poverty, so what were the reasons for this madness? I was in a spider web entanglement, and I couldn't seem to get out.

I believed that with all my strength and knowledge I would someday come out of that dilemma. I know the people in my life at the time obviously thought I was insane. Like Job, during that time, I lost the love of family as I became a burden at times. On top of it all, the Lord was bringing me through a deep wilderness experience for many years into ministry.

If any of you go through similar situations, know that the Lord will allow you to meet all kinds of people during those times. When you have awakened to the sight of the enemy, you will become more conscious of these people, who they are, and where and when they enter into your life. You will begin to question why some people are being placed in front of you. An "awakening" is exactly that, an eye opener. I challenge all of you to ask a man or woman what their motives and intentions are in your life, and I guarantee you most of them will say, "I don't have any." Time will tell.

No matter how you view it, there are always lessons to be learned. Most of us don't view close encounters as lessons, but they are. For instance, you meet someone in a store and you begin to talk with them. Learn to not only talk, but to listen. You will find they may tell you something about themselves, or yourself, from that simple encounter, and that information may help you in some kind of way. I remember my youngest son telling me one day while we were at the supermarket, "Mom, you are always talking to people in the store." I replied, "You never know who may need a smile or a kind word from another person. As long as it doesn't hurt anyone, it's OK." Of course, this point is not for children. I believe that even then, the Holy Spirit was teaching me how to really interact with others, and to know that there were people in worse situations than I was in, and being kind to others helps so much. Truly I knew what it was to be treated unkindly.

God is still in control; everything is a process with Him, and He doesn't always move quickly. While the Holy Spirit is the teacher and orchestrating your life, it may take years before He reveals certain information to you. Don't get discouraged, neither be afraid. You may go through hell, but you're not going to die. The journey may be lonely, but trust God while traveling through the spider web entanglement. Hear what the Lord has to say about the many faces, and hearts of those who set traps for you to be launched into the spider web entanglement: This is evilness at its best:

"Behold the Lord's hand is not shortened at all, that it cannot save, nor His ear dull with deafness, that it cannot hear. But your iniquities have made a separation between you and your God, and your sins have hidden His face from you, so that He will not hear. For your hands are defiled with blood and your fingers with iniquity; your lips have spoken lies, your tongue mutters wickedness. None sues or calls in righteousness (but for the sake of doing injury to others—to take some undue advantage); no one goes to law honestly and pleads (his case) in truth; they trust in emptiness, worthlessness and futility, and speaking lies! They conceive mischief and bring forth evil! They hatch adders' eggs and weave the spider's web; he who eats of their eggs dies, and (from an egg) which is crushed a viper breaks out (for their nature is ruinous, deadly, evil). Their webs will not serve as clothing, nor will they cover themselves with what they make; their works are works of iniquity, and the act of violence is in their hands. Their feet run evil, and they make haste to shed innocent blood. Their

thoughts are thoughts of iniquity; desolation and destruction are in their paths and highways. The way of peace they know not, and there is no justice or right in their goings. They have made them into crooked paths; whoever goes in them does not know peace."

Isaiah 59:1-8

<u>Note: these words speak of the process of deliverance:</u>

He shall come as a Redeemer to Zion and to those in Jacob (Israel) who turns from transgression, says the Lord. As for me, this is my covenant or league with them, says the Lord: My Spirit, Who is upon you (and Who writes the law of God inwardly on the heart), and My words which I have put in your mouth shall not depart out of your mouth, or out of the mouths of your (true, spiritual) children, or out of the mouths of your children's children, says the Lord, from henceforth and forever. Isaiah 59:20-21

Yahweh has all the answers.

Notes to Myself

11

Loneliness

During times of loneliness, I became an emotional wreck. I felt disconnected from everyone around me. Being in that situation practically took over my life, and there were times when I had feelings of despair, being distraught, and not having anyone who really cared about me. There were no friends, no family, and the business I loved was gone. Here I was, a person who once upon a time loved life, enjoyed my life, and loved helping others, and now I was completely in an opposite position. I went from a very high energized person to energy that was at minus zero.

Loneliness was often what I felt. For some reason, it was hard for me to get through one day to another. *Loneliness is a complex and usually unpleasant feeling in which a person feels a strong sense of emptiness and solitude. The causes of loneliness are varied, but it can be affected by social, mental, emotional, and spiritual factors. It is a natural phenomenon, since humans are social creatures by nature. Loneliness has also been described as social pain—a psychological mechanism meant to alert an individual of isolation and motivate him or her to seek social connections.*

If there is one thing I learned is who was for me, and who was against me. It became very clear who was in my corner. At times, some people would say things to me that were very mean and belittling.

Talking about the devil making a person "speak a thing," and we can always count on Satan and his imps to do their job extremely well. They're always on time, but God is still in control.

I tried several times to start a new business, but that never worked. It seemed as though the Lord had zapped me of all my gifts and talents. I was numb. I just couldn't get back into the full swing of things. Whenever, I would go out, my demeanor stated that I was OK, but truly I was not. I was dead inside. Was this how **Job** felt when God was bringing him through his trials? I wouldn't wish this on anyone, not even my worst enemies.

Loneliness gets to the very essence of your soul at times, and will make you want to scream for someone who truly loves you to come to your rescue. When that does not happen, it feels like the world's bottom has fallen out. One thing the Holy Spirit taught me during this time was to "hug myself" and to say myself "I love me." You can surely continue to do this over and over again until the pain subsides. Don't worry; the pain will surely subside, until it's gone away. I am so very glad that the Holy Spirit has taught me so much; and it all has to do with learning to love yourself so you can love others. I had to live.

Loneliness is a "fruit" listed under the stronghold Spirit of Heaviness. Listed are more of these fruits for you to become familiar with, and to overcome if you are in bondage from any of these.

a) Depression: a serious medical condition in which a person feels very sad, hopeless, and unimportant and often is unable to live in a normal way

b) Grief: keen mental suffering or distress over affliction or loss; sharp sorrow; painful regret

c) Sadness: emotional pain associated with, or characterized by feelings of disadvantage

d) Unhappiness: Crying easily, and constantly on the verge of tears

e) Spirit of Deep Sleep: can also be a fruit of Loneliness, feeling overwhelmed

f) Self-Pity: a feeling of pity for yourself because you believe you have suffered more than is fair or reasonable

---

"To console those who mourn in Zion, To give them beauty for ashes, The oil of joy for mourning, The garment of praise for the spirit of heaviness; That they may be called trees of righteousness, the planting of the Lord, that He may be glorified."

Isaiah 61:3

Notes to Myself

12

Lord Where are You?

Although there will always be trials, go through them, never dwell in them. Don't lose the opportunity to reach your destiny.

When we travel through time with life on our heels, and yearning for the best in life, there are moments when we may feel alone, desperate, and unsure of what is going on. These are the times when we should look up into the sky, pull ourselves together, and hold on. Don't be so eager to give in to self-pity and depression. Don't give in to feelings that rob you of the life that the Almighty has for you. If you don't see this thing through, you will never know what you have missed. Don't listen to the old saying, "You will never miss what you never had." Yes you will, because you will always wonder "What if?" Fight, press and pull your way through. Whatever it takes, do it.

No one said it was going to be easy, but endurance wins the victory; patience builds character, courage exudes boldness. There are many times when I cried out to the Lord, "Where are You?" Talk to the Lord about what concerns you.

"The Lord will perfect that which concerns me; Your mercy, O Lord, endures forever; Do not forsake the works of Your hands."

Psalm 138:8

He is your best listener and friend; and the ironic thing is that He will send the Holy Spirit to soothe your pain, and put the best Band-Aide on the spot where it hurts. He is God all by Himself. He can touch you where no human being can touch. He can whisper in your ear like no human being ever will. And, you can always rely on the fact that whatever He tells you, you will never go wrong, if you are obedient. Trust God; have faith in Him.

Trials come to build upon that which is already inside of you. Trials come to teach you that you can overcome hurt, pain, poverty, and anything else that comes against you. Remember, no weapon formed against you shall prosper. God said so, and it is what it is. Make up your mind that nothing is going to stop you from getting what belongs to you. There were many times when I felt like giving up, and I would go to my wall and cry out to the Lord. There were many times when I wouldn't, or couldn't talk to those who were around me. Why? I needed my space. I needed my space to talk to the Lord and to hear His voice. You can't hear God when there is a lot of noise all around you. Even now, there are times when I just want to be alone with absolutely no intrusions.

Sometimes, you may have to take time and be alone, away from everyone that is close to you. These are times when you need to be in God's presence all by yourself. Until others get to understand this, there may be some misunderstandings about it, or perhaps, a lack of acceptance from others. Don't allow any human being on this earth to get between you and God. Even if you feel in love, if that person does not step up to the plate, then they are not the one. The truth is the light. I realize everyone is not on the same level, but guess what? You can get there. When both parties are on the same level in God, then all is well. Being unevenly yoked hinders the Holy Spirit from doing a good work in you.

God may pull us into our prayer closet to be with Him only; then we can wait on Him and hear His voice. The Holy Spirit will show up; as He directs, He instructs, He comforts, He guides, and not everything is always "right now." His message (s) may be for a later time. But one thing is for sure: He will always inform you of the timing. My understanding in hearing from God is that He does not answer my questions when my answers are "No," or if it's not the right time. God is amazing; through revelation knowledge, He gives us timing. Isn't that great? Your desire may be right now, but God may take care of those desires at a later time. In the meantime, delight yourself in the greatness of the Lord Jesus Christ.

During the many years of, trials and tribulations, I still felt as though I was stuck in a spider web entanglement. Every time I thought I was out, I was pulled back in, and each time was worse than the last. So much was going on. It still took many more years for me to make it through. All the time I was going through long suffering, I still received more of God.

"*And He said, "Listen, all of you of Judah and you inhabitants of Jerusalem, and you, King Jehoshaphat! Thus says the Lord to you: "Do not be afraid nor dismayed because of this great multitude, for the battle is not yours, but God's."*
2 Chronicles 20:15

Notes to Myself

13

Blessing Blockers

When you are traveling the road to your destiny, blessing blockers will intrude in your life. The blessing blockers I am speaking of are people or things that are sent to meet you in your life for a specific reason (s). These people will attach themselves to you for their own good, not yours. They will breathe the air you breathe, eat the food you eat, act like they're your best friend, smile when you smile, laugh when you laugh, and may even cry when you cry sometimes. But one day, strange things begin to happen, and so it may seem to you. All of a sudden, you begin to see another side of this person. Their actions change toward you; they may begin to say things that are completely opposite of the kind of relationship you thought you had with this person. They will begin to speak things that are the complete opposite of how you're thinking, and do things that are not as you would like them to be done. Don't forget, blessing blockers are sent into your life to take your eyes off the prize that God has for you. Remember, whenever you're going through changes in your life, you are very vulnerable.

These people are distractions that are sent by the enemy to block your blessings. The devil is always on his job. A distraction is someone or something that will turn your eye away from your purpose; keeping your mind occupied and focused on another agenda. And before you know it, disobedience on your part occurs. Disobedience toward God is a big blessing blocker. Remember the devil can't do anything to you unless God gives him permission.

During my trials, the spirit that began walking with me was once again, the jezebel spirits. They are controlling, they always have motives and intentions for everything, and jealous hearts. These people become the jealous hearted, devious grudge holding individuals that can no longer contain themselves. Stuff begins to come out of their mouths that you can't believe. Soon you will wonder if you're crazy or is there some type of demonic force going on around you. Believe me, there is a demonic force. Demonic forces of evil, trying to always steer you in the wrong direction.

There is one thing I know for sure; you can't change a jealous heart. That is a God job, for sure. By that point, God had stripped me of everything I owned, my life was completely flipped upside down, so believe me, I was definitely looking for relief from somewhere, but there was none. I kept meeting these jezebel spirits who would always want to give me things, such as finances, etc. But you need to be still and see that for what it really is. These people already exhibit behavior that they don't like you, but here's the trick: they are really looking at you as some poor lost pitiful soul that can't help yourself, while they secretly gloat behind your back. In their warped minds, they truly believe they are the ones that will save you from destitution, and then they will be able to say "If it wasn't for me, you would not have made it." God will not allow that to happen.

If you recall, Abraham had a similar situation in rescuing Lot from the four kings who took over the land of Sodom and Gomorrah, and afterward the King of Sodom said to Abram "Give me the people and keep the goods for yourself." *"But Abraham said to the king of Sodom, I have lifted up my hand and sworn to the Lord, God Most High, the Possessor and Maker of heaven and earth. That I would not take a thread or a shoelace or anything that is yours, lest you should say, I have made Abram rich."*

Genesis 14:22-23

The Lord made me realize that there are people you will not want to receive anything from, nor will He allow you to eat with these people. Be careful whom you keep company with; ask God for discernment of their spirits, and then you will be able to deal with them accordingly. No matter how bad things are, Jesus reveals and gives discernment that is beyond your understanding.

If you have not met anyone like the king or my former encounters, at some point in time, perhaps there will be someone in your life that will think they are the one (s) who will help you comeback into prosperity after you have fallen. However, I pray that does not happen to you.

"But remember the Lord your God, for it is he who gives you the ability to produce wealth, and so confirms his covenant, which he swore to your forefathers, as it is this day."

Deuteronomy 8:18

As you can see, God is the one who gives us the power to get wealth. Your gifts should be stirring up as you read this book. Don't sit on your gifts. God did not give them to you to become dormant. Be brave, get excited. The Spirit of the Lord is speaking to you.

Another version of blessing blockers are those that enter your life to make you become disobedient to the will of God. In *1Kings 13,* the Lord sent a prophet out to do the work of God, and told him as reiterated in *vs. 9 "For so was it commanded by the word of the Lord, You shall eat no bread or drink water or return by the way you came."* If you continue to read farther, you will find in vs. 18, that a second prophet convinced him that he too was a prophet; the man misled him. *"He answered I am a prophet also, as you are. And an angel spoke to me by the word of the Lord, saying; Bring him back with you to your house, that he may eat bread and drink water. But he lied to him. "So the man from Judah went back with him and ate and drank water in his house."*

1Kings 13:18-19

Further down in the scriptures you will see that the prophet from Judah left the man's house and began his journey once again; a lion came upon him and his donkey and killed the first prophet. People passed the poor man on the road and did nothing to dispose of his body. Finally, the prophet came and buried him in his own grave and told his sons to bury his bones next to the man when he died, for surely, the first prophet's spoken words would come true. This was more of Jeroboam, the king's deception and lies. Surely, if one viewed the grave in later years, and both set of bones were there, how would you know which bones belonged to whom? Lies and deception.

1 Kings 13, is full of lies, deception, disobedience to the command of the Lord, and finally death. It is a must that we know who we are following, who we are taking commands from, and the purpose of those commands. If you can believe that the Lord is in control of your life's situations, then your blessings will not be blocked. The crust of these scriptures is *"the turning away from what the Lord has spoken to you to do."* It's not always easy to follow the voice of God, and more so, to be obedient to His voice. It's easy to turn away and do the opposite from His command; however, much will be lost because of your disobedience.

You know your relationship with the Father, and if you have not built a relationship with God, there is no better time than right now. His voice will teach you whatever you need to hear, to walk in His will and His way. After reading this information, I am sure many will agree there is a lot more to know about the Father. If you become unsure of hearing the voice of God, go back to Him and ask for clarity. He will give it to you.

If you have no other choice but to stand alone; **STAND!**

"Therefore take up the whole armor of God, that you may be able to withstand in the evil day, and having done all, to stand."

Ephesians 6:13

Notes to Myself

14

Thieving Spirit –

Americanized Slavery

During these times, my judgment became off centered in what God had planned for me, and what I wanted for myself. I wanted so badly to move from the northern part of the state where I lived, and return to the southern part of the state. I took a public service type of position a hundred miles round trip per day from my home believing that if I took the job, I would eventually return to that area. It was one of the worst mistakes I've ever made. Or was this in God's plan to make me realize I didn't call the shots for my life. When God has a plan, and you are "called" by Him, there's no getting around it, your plans will not work, no matter what you try to do.

During this time I felt as though I was gliding through from day to day. An old friend of mind was a supervisor at that job, and referred me for the position. After our initial training, we had to go through another training once starting the job. After being there for two weeks, my supervisor (male) said something to me that he should not have. I told my friend and she said "You should definitely go to management about that. The manager will not tolerate that kind of behavior." Going to management did not work out the way my friend said it would, and it back fired on me. The manager began to treat me as if I had done something wrong. My friend left me holding the bag all alone, and then she stopped coming by my desk to see me as she had done prior to the incident.

Now, here's the kicker about that job. They started us out with a certain hourly payment plan each week, then within a couple of months, my coworkers and I were put on a plan that I still do not understand. Part of the salaries would depend on whether we made mistakes while inputting data into the computer system. If we made mistakes, a certain figure would be deducted from our normal weekly pay, whatever that was supposed to be. Again, I still don't understand the system, or how much money I really made. I can guarantee you it wasn't very much at all. The ironic thing was that the company leaders never told us during training or otherwise how this system really worked. I was once told that it definitely was not working on a commission basis. Many years later, I spoke with someone that had been working there part time for six years while in college, and she said "they never gave her a raise."

Because I did not understand the meaning of the system the company had set up, one day I asked the Holy Spirit "what is this system about?" As surely as I am writing this book, the Holy Spirit immediately spoke and said **"A Thieving Spirit – Americanized Slavery."** Well, how do you like that? First, let me say, that the Lord does not always speak quickly when you ask Him a question. However, in this case, He spoke so quickly it seemed I hardly got the question out of my mouth before He responded. I immediately knew that job was also a plan of God's, although originally I thought I had made a mistake by taking the position.

So, in other words, the company set up a system whereby their return on investment would include part of the employees' salaries, because any mistake an employee made would be taken from their weekly pay. I knew I had to get out of there. I was working at a job where I traveled three hours per day, one hundred miles round trip on my car, and an employer who sought to find mistakes in every keystroke and daily activity of my work so that they could deduct dollars from my weekly pay. Can anyone see the madness in this other than me? Truly, I believe the Holy Spirit allowed me to do this so that the world can see how unfair this was. This is being done in the United States of America you all, not some third world country. Right here in the good old USA, under your nose, and people are doing this every day. Leaders in this company are walking away with seven figure incomes, and perks to the max every year; and their employees have to worry about whether they make a typo. We read about some large companies getting away with practically anything all the time, but it makes everything much clearer when you've actually worked in this type of environment.

A few months after I started working there, the company leaders proposed a little incentive plan to see how many people would reach their monthly averages without making little or no mistakes. This was insane to say the least; now we were all put into a contest. I just wanted out of there.

One day I asked one of the managers, "How did this pay system come about?" I was told it was put into effect by a former employee, and obviously, the company owners liked it. I was also told that the person who initially implemented the procedure was no longer there, because he had been terminated because of embezzlement. It's no wonder the Holy Spirit told me **"A Thieving Spirit."** I was not surprised upon getting that word. And, why wouldn't the owners like it? This system meant more money in their pockets. This is America, and at the time, I was surprised to know that such a system existed. I guarantee the CEOs, Presidents, Vice Presidents and Managers were not working on that system. It would seem to me that the managers would get some sort of incentive if their employees did well in this working environment.

It's awesome when the Holy Spirit is taking you through on your journey. The amount of information you can obtain from various sources is unimaginable. This was truly a journey to write about both to benefit others and to glorify God. **Awesome!**

As always, my main goal was to get out of there, and I didn't care what it took. I just wanted out. And so a door opened and I walked through it.

I was finally learning to reason with and understand the weird life I was living. I was in training. When the Holy Spirit is training you, there is no end to what may occur and how you will go through situations in your life. Everything is being orchestrated by Him who loves you so much. Trust me, things are not always good. There are going to be hurdles, falls, pain, anger, lack of trust issues, and the lying spirit is always going to come up in leaps and bounds. When the heat is turned up, expect anything to happen in a matter of seconds.

Below is a list of the "fruits" of the **Lying Spirit** that was in operation at that company.

a) *Manipulation: to adapt or change (accounts, figures, etc.) to suit one's purpose or advantage.*

b) *Deceit: making or trying to make someone believe something that is not true.*

c) *Hypocrisy: The practice of professing beliefs, feelings, or virtues that one does not hold or possess; falseness.*

Spirit of Haughtiness:

a) *Entitlement: the company helping themselves to part of the employees' salaries*

Notes to Myself

15

Pride and Arrogance

Believe me; I thought this was a great door to walk through. God allows us to walk into doors that will train us to be humble, loving, kind and dislike a person all at the same time. This time I walked into a Christian business. The owner and his human resource manager had a long conversation with me during the interview process, and everything seemed to have worked out well. I was expecting to give the former employer notice; however, the new company I interviewed with called in two days and stated that the owner needed me to start right away because of a project they were working on; so I cut my time short and gladly left the former employer that was farther away.

There are some people that become prideful, arrogant, and pumped up like an inflatable balloon. Their sense of pride is so high that when they fall down, they're like Humpty Dumpty sat on the wall; Humpty Dumpty had a great fall. In their minds, they believe that it's alright to mistreat people, and to say whatever they want to say to you, whenever they want. And to top it off, they continue to smile and converse with you as if nothing happened. Can it get any worse than that? Imagine the mind-set of arrogance and pride to expect someone to work for you for free when the worker is supposed to have a job, not a hobby. Unfortunately, these are some of the traits of some leaders who have forgotten that the world owes them nothing.

When people work for a company, it simply means they should be getting paid on payday. If you haven't set up a contract to not receive payment for your services, you should get paid. In the central cities of the United States, we are not working in a system of enslavement, but there are certainly many companies that operate this way on a daily basis. Although paychecks have diminished quite a bit, I am sure the workers do not want to be enslaved.

Here I was in the same old type of situation again. I thought to myself, what more can happen to me while my life continues to spiral downward? At that time, I was already desperate. I realized life could deal you a full deck of confusing cards, you will wonder if you're going crazy at times. Actually, you are not going crazy, it just seems that way when it comes to walking into your destiny.

I actually took the job referred by Michele, someone I knew from the past, although prior to our meeting, I had not seen her for many years. However, everything seemed well and I thought life was finally going to be OK. Things begin to happen when people see that your life has not been dormant as they would have hoped or thought. I showed Michele my first book, and she became my arch enemy. It's sad when some people cannot be happy for you.

Moving forward in my responsibilities, I realized this was the time for me to meet more people involved in this Christian business. I wanted to understand the people I was working for, so I begin to attend some of their festivities. It didn't take but a very short time span for the boss to reveal himself, and all the mess that was going on in the office, and so I had been hired under false pretenses, lies and deception. Lord have mercy. I was actually lured from my old position to take this one, all to find, there was no paycheck. Three weeks before payroll, the company didn't have enough money to pay the staff, even though they hired me. That was pure outright deception.

Now, this is how this type of situation works. The boss was walking in pride and arrogance, abusive and very cynical. Unfortunately, the employees did not receive pay checks in previous weeks, and no one did anything about it. They received nothing but promises, and unfortunately, they kept on working for free, hoping that one day the boss would live up to his word. I was told this was the way this person did business.

With this position, if it had been true; I would have been able to have my own place again, and live comfortably. However, the entire interview, hiring me, everything was a lie. Can you imagine? In the long run, it took me three months to get paid for the weeks I worked there; and it was unbelievable how the boss tried to lie and give me less money than I should have gotten. It seemed there was no end to this person's madness. However; from my past experiences, I knew all the things I had to do to get my money; and so, I went after him.

This was pride and arrogance at its' best. He was so self-righteous that he thought it was OK to call me, and go through the motions of me listening to his lying, and holier-than-thou behavior on the phone. He sent me two checks with two different bank names, and neither of them was worth the ink on the paper. He even told me that because his business was a nonprofit organization, employees got taxed differently; therefore, the amount I stated to him that he owed me would be less. I did not respond to his nonsense, except to tell him not to call me again, and just send the money.

It took three months and some strength I didn't know I had; however, he was revealed to all the right people that have rules and regulations on people's wages and such. I went directly to the Department of Labor, Wages and Hours, and filed a complaint against him. The department has forms you can complete that explains all the documentation to be submitted with your complaint. I also went to a lawyer and had him write a letter to the business, so that my check would be forwarded directly to the lawyer, and I would have no further contact with him or his office. It is not necessary to go to a lawyer and the wages and hours department; it was my choice. However, in this case, both of them worked out simultaneously, and I received my money.

I was so amazed to find out that some people had been working there for many years and living through the madness. Dedicated people will sometimes do the most unusual things, even to the point of being pimped by a boss. How sad is that, and they know they're being pimped? Manipulation, control, and speaking softly with a ruthless spirit are more traits of jezebels, walking in the stronghold Spirit of Haughtiness.

It's also amazing to see how these kinds of people operate, robbing you of everything you have, and claiming in the name of Jesus that they're helping you or someone else. Actually, they're not helping anyone but themselves. As the word says, we should all do things in love, *"That we should no longer be children, tossed to and fro and carried about with every wind of doctrine, by the trickery of men, in the cunning craftiness of deceitful plotting."*

Ephesians 4:14

Again, when people are close to the leader and they're under control of the jezebel spirit, their life stops. I felt like they were in a deep sleep, and I wanted to yell "Wake up." But they kept on sleeping. It is so sad to see how some people can believe in mankind so much, that they begin to think it's OK to be abused. The unfortunate thing is they usually don't know they are being abused, because they believe man, particularly when the man is a Christian leader. God does not want us to be a slave to anyone or anything.

One of the saddest things about this is there are so many leaders in ministry who believe they can walk all over people, abuse and misuse them, especially financially, and they continue to get away with this, because people allow it to happen.

Now in the process of all this, someone actually said to me, "We're not supposed to sue other Christians." I can tell you that I call a spade, a spade, and do not make shortcuts for anyone who is literally trying to pull one over on me, and rob me up close while crying out, "Jesus, Jesus, Jesus." Are you serious? Let's be real, the world is full of false leaders, and the like, so if you stand for nothing, you will fall for anything. I know that the God I serve will not have me operate in blindness to those who are deceiving me. Once my eyes are opened wide, I tell it like it is. Unfortunately for the young lady that stated "We're not supposed to sue other Christians", I said to her, "I'm suing the devil for thinking he can rob me. Call it whatever you want." She had a perfect mindset to be pimped. Everything that looks like gold is not gold. Serve God, not mankind. There is a great difference.

People of God, these are some terrible times that we are living in, and if you don't get discernment and revelation from the word of God; you will be lost in all the false information that some people are bringing forth. You need to be cognizant of the word of God for yourself. Times have changed, but the Word of God has not changed. We need a wake-up call in the things of God. One of the best things that happened in this case is that the labor board found out about the unethical things the employer was doing to the employees.

Here we find the stronghold Spirit of Haughtiness which includes the "fruits" of lies, egotistical, entitlement, arrogance, proud, pride, and stubbornness. There are other "fruits" in this category; however, stay in the presence of God, and He will reveal so many things to you.

a) Lies: a false statement made with deliberate intent to deceive; an intentional untruth.

b) Strong Delusion: a belief held with strong conviction despite superior evidence to the contrary.

c) Egotistical egoism: Someone who is egotistical is full of himself; completely self-absorbed.

d) Controlling: To exercise authoritative or dominating influence over others; direct.

e) Self-righteousness: having or showing a strong belief that your own actions, opinions, etc., are right and others are wrong.

f) Entitlement: the condition of having a right to have, do, or get something. the feeling or belief that you deserve to be given something (such as special privileges)

All the ways of a man are pure in his own eyes; But the Lord weighs the spirits.

Proverbs 16:2

Notes to Myself

16

A Walk With Jesus

Oh, Lord, I am so tired. At that point I had lost everything. I couldn't pay rent, utilities, car note–all hell had broken loose in my life. It was total disruption; and my life was falling apart. I eventually lost my apartment, and had to live with others, which became an absolute nightmare. Does anyone know what it's like to live in another person's home? Lord, have mercy. But even on this journey, God showed me some things. When the Father takes you on a journey, He will flip your life upside down, and allow you to travel on roads that lead to a "book of knowledge, wisdom, discernment, understanding, humbleness, and revelations" all at the same time, and in the name of love.

Now this is what I found out when God allowed me to live in other people's homes. You can discuss what you have, and make an agreement, but that doesn't matter because sooner or later it will all change in their eyes to more money. But there's one ingredient that is missing in the beginning, no matter what you've discussed prior to the living arrangements, "motives" and "intentions" will eventually show up, and not in your favor. Once everyone's true colors begin to show, you may find your unwanted self out on your behind. There is not enough love in the world when a person has motives and intentions that differ from the original spoken ones. Remember, the original reason was always money, but you're not supposed to know that.

God puts us all to a test to see how we're all going to treat each other. The problem is the Christian providers usually don't realize they're being tested by God as well as you. So, the saga begins. As time goes on, conflicts begin to materialize, and at that point, all hell breaks loose.

One of the most important things the Holy Spirit taught me is how to become "humble." Humbling myself without being angry was very complicated, but the Holy Spirit took me through trials and tests, teaching me how to walk in "all truth" simultaneously.

During one of these awesome moments when I was alone with God, I cried out to Him and asked why He was taking me through this maze. In that still, small voice He replied, **"You have been walking with Jesus."** I fell to my knees and worshiped, cried, and spoke in my heavenly language until I was weak. I had been walking with Jesus, and all of a sudden I could see Jesus. I saw Him as He was being tortured, beaten, spat upon, humiliated, abused, carrying his own cross, and then crucified. I realized if He had to go through all that, for me, then so did I. All that abuse was making me into the woman God wanted me to be. I asked Him for that some years earlier and never imagined it would be this way.

Walking with Jesus meant God was allowing me to be in front of a person who manifested unclean spirits. There would be obscene language flared at me, facial expression changes to obvious anger; and then the Lord would actually have me turn around and pray for that person during my prayer time. Obviously, this is the kind of behavior that I would say "Father, what are you doing?" In the end, I did it anyway. When you are walking in the will and way of God, you do things that may seem a little strange at first. Know that God is steadily teaching you how to love unconditionally.

During this time and dealing with my awkward experiences, my Father would still teach me to have that "agape" love in spite of what I had endured. I began to see the pain, hurt, fear, manipulation, deception, control, and anger as the unclean spirits engulfed the other person's state of mind. Through my growing in agape love, I wanted to help them so much because I knew the person was really sick, and I wanted them to be well.

Loving a person unconditionally is seeing them as God sees them, with love. This does not mean that you allow anyone to abuse you to the extent that removes you from being who you are as a person and your spiritual well-being. Your spiritual well-being is an absolute necessity for the Holy Spirit to bring you through these troubling times. But, you also have a responsibility to others' well-being as well. First, and foremost, your responsibility is to help others in their Christian growth. But when there are demonic forces, you need to remove yourself from the dwelling before you get hurt.

"Let no one seek his own, but each one, the other's well being. Then, this will be all to the glory of God."

1 Corinthian 10:24

No one could have told me twenty years ago that I would have gone through all these trials and tribulations. I had my life sort of planned out. I certainly did not know anything about a walk with Jesus. Notice, I had my life planned. But God's plan for my life was absolutely different from anything I ever dreamed of.

So, I had been walking with Jesus and still had a long way to go. Awesome.

Notes to Myself

17

Healing

Talk about emotional pain, such as feeling unloved, abandoned, rejected, etc. These are all signs of deep rooted predispositions. Predispositions mean, "a liability or tendency to suffer from a particular condition, hold a particular attitude, or act in a particular way." Lord knows, I had a lot going on. Healing takes a long time; nothing just happens overnight. When we are dealing with the psychological, inner depths of our mind, there is a process to moving into complete wellness and wholeness.

At times, I would say to the Lord, "Please take my mind back." I was in so much pain. I needed to be "free." I was at a point where I didn't know what to do, where to turn; I felt paralyzed. I felt a loss of empowerment, I had no motivation, and I felt helpless, tired, and drained of all my strength. I cried out. I can truly say that I know how it must have felt to my ancestors to be enslaved. I felt enslaved in my own being.

I couldn't keep my mind on anything I tried to do. But, I knew there must have been some very important reasons why I was going through all the mess I was enduring, but I didn't have any answers.

Healing, what's that? Can you imagine the "stuff" that you carry inside when there's so much pain, and you don't know what to do with it? I am sure if you could look inside yourself, there would probably be a stomach and heart full of mush. To say nothing of what your mind looks like; all those brain cells looking like worms crawling around in your head. A time for healing is a need for all of us, to be whole in every area of our lives. Healing of the heart is where we all need to ultimately be. There is so many unclean spirits that enter into our hearts through the years of our lives, and even before we are born. We may carry residue from our mom and dad, and the issues they were carrying before you were born.

As I enter into the lives of many, I see so much pain, brokenness, instability, and the desire to control everything and everybody. Many people do not address these types of issues in their personal lives, because they don't think anything is wrong. As far as they are concerned, they're living a healthy lifestyle. And those that know their lives aren't stable sometimes refuse to move forth to have a clean bill of health in their spirit.

I once heard a young woman state that she has abandonment issues, but believes that she will always have them. I beg to differ. In this state of mind, this woman will always have a problem with a man leaving her, children leaving her, and other attachments she may have in her life. There are solutions to that problem. We don't have to live a life consumed with abandonment issues and other unclean spirits. God has a remedy for everything. It is the will of God for all of us to live wholesome and fruitful lifestyles.

The healing process can be a very eye opening experience, probably earth- shaking for some; however, to be free from the issues of life that plague us to live free, healthy, and wise in our minds, hearts, and spirits is so worth the time and effort involved to do so. We should all strive to become good parents, live in and have great relationships, and build the foundation for our lives in a way that is lasting and secure. To be healed means having peace and joy in our lives that leaves an openness in our hearts to attract the right people, where there may have been times when the wrong types of people would enter our hearts, minds, and spirits, and we would usually end up in a painful relationship.

"Behold, I will bring it health and healing; I will heal them and reveal to them the abundance of peace and truth."

Jeremiah 33:6

Notes to Myself

18

Sometimes I Cry

Like Jeremiah the crying prophet, Sometimes I Cry
I Cry for Myself at times,
I Cry for Others at times,
When I see sad hearts and the pain they carry
I Cry,
I Cry for this Nation.
Oh Lord, stop the Tears from Crying, Crying, Crying.
There are tears of sadness, tears of happiness, and tears of joy.

Many times the Crying becomes Tears no more.

Where did that come from? I don't know, but obviously, my Father wanted me to write it? It is done. Someone needs it.

Often times I cry for even my enemies particularly, as I see them in a situation of unbelief. Once upon a time, I thought I was crying for myself, but Jesus revealed to me that it was not tears for myself, but tears for my enemies as He revealed their aching hearts to me. Jesus said "Sometimes people who live a sinful life do not allow themselves to cry; therefore, someone has to cry for them."

Imagine having a heart that is so hardened, tears do not fall when they need to. My God, I can't imagine it. All the stuff that remains inside, and the inability to release the pain, must be over whelming at times. I don't know about you, but crying helps me feel better, sometimes angry, but I always feel some sense of relief. Our Father knew what He was doing when He gave us tears.

God would not have given us a way to cry, tear ducts, and the like if it was not necessary for us to cry. He wants us to cry in times of pain and times of happiness. It's OK to cry. I know there's an old saying, "Don't let them see you cry;" but you know what, "Let them see you cry." Release in the name of Jesus. Crying is also a way of cleansing your soul. Let the water flow.

I was watching a documentary on John F. Kennedy, Jr., and it stated that their father always told them to never cry; however, when JFK died, Joe Kennedy (JFK's father) cried. So, you see, sometimes we can't help but to cry; God knows when it is necessary, even if we do not.

"But may the God of all grace, who called us to His eternal glory by Christ Jesus, after you have suffered a while, perfect, establish, strengthen, and settle you."

1Peter 5:10

Notes to Myself

19

Christians Co-Signing Lying Spirits

Many say they are Christians but act otherwise. The Bible talks about Christians lying in many different venues. This can be focused on several avenues, particularly Christians who are on and off, up and down, confused, and not sure which god they are serving. These people usually agree with the Bible's truths of a situation but if their friends disagree with the truth or tell a lie, they submit themselves to that lie. We've all seen this done, so many times. Yes, all of us should have wisdom about the things of God, but unfortunately, some are so far removed that they think and speak from both sides of their mouth.

We should stand for the truth regardless of situations or circumstances surrounding an issue. An old saying states, "If you don't stand for something, you will fall for anything."

One must be girded with strength to stand for the truth. It's not always pleasant, it doesn't always feel good, and many people will be disappointed in you from time to time. There will be many days when you feel alone, abandoned, neglected, alienated, and not a part of the "in crowd." God is no respecter of persons, so why do so many Christians think it's OK to say "yes, Lord" sometimes, and "no Lord" at other times? I believe the bottom line is that many people do not fear God.

Fearing God has a "yes Lord" mentality all the time. These people stand for the truth all the time; they believe in doing the right thing for the sake of others all the time. They don't stray left and right, but look forward keeping their eyes on Jesus. **James 1:6-8** talks about the doubting, double-minded man.

"But let him ask in faith, with no doubting, for he who doubts is like a wave of the sea driven and tossed by the wind. For let not that man suppose that he will receive anything from the Lord; he is a double-minded man, unstable in all his ways."

James 1:6-8

And so the same goes for those who choose to cosign lies. Cosigning lies basically means agreeing with a person who is telling a lie you are in essence cosigning that lie as if you were actually notarizing the lie. Sometimes, many of you can be put in vicarious situations particularly when you are on your job and if you don't agree and lie; then you may get lied on and lied to. Amen

Doing the will of God only gets easier when you continually walk in His will and His way. Practice makes perfect. All Christians should not entertain a "lying spirit" but for some that's probably easier said than done.

I remember how I felt as I listened to a lying spirit speak to me about a project they were going to work on, but stated they had never done it before. Unfortunately, the person was lying because I had seen them doing this many times prior to our discussion. I felt like running away from him as fast as possible. If a person lies when they don't have to lie, believe me they will lie about anything. That's a dangerous lying spirit, and a bad environment to work in. Life is full of surprises, with unclean evil spirits running rampant; they will devour you at the drop of a dime.

In *Matthew 5:32-37* Jesus talks about swearing under oath; however, we all know that Jesus does not want us to lie at all.

"But let your "Yes" be "Yes", and your "No," "No." For whatever is more than these is from the evil one."

Matthew 5:37

Therefore, the "word" is saying, don't be a luke warm Christian, and don't be double minded. Lying spirits are dangerous; if they lied about something very small in nature, they will lie about you and to you in a big way, particularly in the workplace.

Notes to Myself

20

His Grace

All during these years of torture and trying to redeem myself, the Holy Spirit was leading me into ministry. Being led by the Holy Spirit, I was able to execute women's conferences, teaching and preaching; but there was still more the Father had for me. So, I was still in the Holy Spirit school, and moons away from the mandate being complete that was preordained for my life. I had to learn more about the ministry He was entrusting me with. He guided, directed, revealed, and opened doors to get exactly what I needed at all times. I am still at awe how He does everything. No one can do you, or me, like Jesus.

The gifts that he has given me began to spring forth, my knowledge, wisdom, revelations, discernment, and understandings are all for His glory. As He takes me from one assignment to another; His instructions are endless. Everything always works out just the way He intended them too. The security I feel in Him is like nothing I have experienced before in life, and I am sure I never will from mankind. As I follow His lead, the teachings never stop. I've learned to do the most important things in life in "His timing," as the Holy Spirit once told me, "He orchestrates my life." I say Yes Lord.

I realize that it is through God's Grace while I am moving forward in the vicissitudes of life, and whatever my divine destiny, it is surely purposed by my Father. *"Grace" has been defined as "the love and unmerited favor given to us by God because God desires us to have it, not because of anything we have done to earn it."* He has his Grace upon me with all the changes I have been through, yet standing as secure as the days are long. Although many times I have thought of and felt like death knocking at my door; yet He continues to bless me with his unmerited favor.

The Lord has shown me that the "remnants" will hold fast to the things of God and will not stumble moving forward while walking in His will and His way. This is a crucial time for the sons of God. So many will have to make decisions particularly regarding gay marriages that will make many Christians very uncomfortable; however, there should be no pain if you are sure of who you serve and can sustain the persecutions before you. Oh, you will be tested beyond measure. Some of you will have to decide openly who and what you stand for. The pressures of life's intrusions are upon us. *Intrusions are deliberate moves into someone else's territory, either literal or figurative. Intrusions are also inappropriate or unwelcomed additions.*

There will be no more church as usual. Leaders in the church will have to make decisions many of them never thought they would have to make; however, this will be a true test of their faith going forward. Congregation members will have to make decisions whether they will stay or go. Sons of God, His grace is upon you, but making the right decisions to stand on the word of God is crucial. If you believe that the government is your provider, then the trust you should have in God is already null and void. Decide to earn His grace that He has freely given you; perhaps, it is time for payback.

"For by grace you have been saved through faith, and that not Of yourselves, it is the gift of God, not of works, lest anyone should boast. For we are workmanship, created in Christ Jesus for good works, which God prepared beforehand that we should walk in them."

Ephesians 5:8-10

Notes to Myself

21

The Spirit of Jealousy

One of the nasty, ugly spirits I have encountered is the "stronghold Spirit of Jealousy." And when a person is wearing the "Spirit of Jealousy" you can believe that the victim is going to encounter many unclean spiritual attacks. I encountered the "fruits of anger, rage, and creating division" by a former manager whose jealousy could not be hidden. However, when you are wearing these unclean spirits, it is complicated to keep them hidden.

Early on I hosted a radio talk program, and I discussed a topic on jealousy and envy. After some research in the bible, I found many scriptures relating to these spirits. The information below will give you the opportunity to see what God had to say about these unclean spirits.

Jealousy and Envy

Jealousy: is the uneasiness felt due to suspicion, resentment or fear of rivalry, especially in regards to love or affection.

" Now Israel loved Joseph more than all his children, because he was the son of his old age. Also, he made him a tunic of many colors. But when his brothers saw that their father loved him more than all his brothers, they hated him and could not speak peaceably to him. "

Genesis 37:3-4

Here, we see Joseph's brothers and their jealousy, which explains how deep the consciousness is of the individuals carrying jealousy, envy, resentment, hatred, malice in their hearts, and it determines how deadly that can be.

What did Joseph do many years later? He forgave his brothers, brought them out of poverty, and didn't tell his father, Israel, what the brothers had done, although the brothers tried to kill him years before. Actually they left him for dead. He showed them much love. His acts of kindness were from God.

Envy: a feeling of discontent and resentment aroused by and in conjunction with desire for the possessions, position, success, or qualities of another. The desire to have for oneself something possessed by another is covetousness.

So in other words, envying a person can put you in such a state of mind, that if you desire something another person has, you can eventually envy them to the point of no return. WOW! People of God, that's pretty deep... The point of no return only comes under submission to God.

Sons of God, make no mistake about it, there are some people who want to take your place. I once thought this only happened when you had some clout, status, or a few things going on with yourself, but not so. You can be penniless, but obviously, there are some things that some people just wish they had, and you have it. We can return to "a person envying your qualities."

Now, here are some of the things I found out when I was going through the wilderness, and people still did not like me. I didn't have to do anything to them. Please don't view this information as boasting, but I mention it here to give you more insight into how jealousy can infiltrate a person's life, although there is nothing to be jealous about, or so I thought.

1) Even if I was broke with no money in my pocket; I always looked like I had something
2) "No clichés in the church." Lord I will not be a part of clichés
3) I carried myself in the highest esteem,

4) Looking good, although I felt so bad
5) I treated people nice, and I smiled, even when I knew they hated me
6) I was still fashionable with old clothes on, but nobody knew it
7) I had confidence in myself – (a main ingredient)
8) Last, but not least, carry and wear the Anointing God has placed on my life. We can't forget that some Christians are jealous of your anointing, as if, you are responsible for giving that to yourself

Jealousy, envy, hatred, malice, and resentment, are all "heart issues." No matter what is going on. Even though you know the person envies you or has jealousy in their heart against you we as believers are supposed to treat others with love no matter what is going on. Jealousy, envy, hatred, malice, and resentment, all come from a carnal state of mind, and unless the person becomes saved, the mind will not become transformed. There must be transformation and renewing of the mind.

As the Holy Spirit began to bring me into ministry, He whispered to me one day and said, "Study the heart scriptures." I said, "Why does he want me to study the heart scriptures?" However, being obedient, I began to study them. I found there are many scriptures that talk about Jesus meeting many different people while He was ministering, and each time "their hearts were revealed to Him." No matter what they say to you let me assure you, that you too can read the hearts of man.

"But I make known to you, brethren, that the gospel which was preached by me is not according to man.…For I neither received it from man, nor was I taught it, but it came through the revelation of Jesus Christ."

Galatians 1:11-12

Ask Jesus for more and more revelations and discernment of the spirits of whom you are keeping company with. Some people are sent to teach you a lesson (s) for some future activities in your walk with God, while others come to distract you from your ministry. Others may come to deliver a word. There may be many reasons "people are sent your way." However, you need to know that you must keep seeking revelation from Jesus Christ, and soon he will show you. Amen. Once you know who you are walking with, you will then know how to handle the encounters you have with these people. Truly, they will not know what you know. Because you will continue to show love, their intent is to one day send you into a tailspin. Watch the Father, the son and the Holy Spirit keep you grounded, and composed while they're going through.

Sons and daughters of God, there are so many scriptures in the word that talks about our hearts. Out of the heart comes the issues of life and if you don't believe it, spend some time with a person that envies you; spend some time with someone that is jealous of you, hates you, resents you, etc. I guarantee you that one day they are going to speak something out of their heart that may shock you and them. They will look very silly, but it's going to materialize. Believe and receive that! Actually, what happens is they can't contain themselves so one day they will suddenly lose it, and out of their mouths will come those nasty words, tones, behavioral changes towards you. I've seen it many times.

"As in water face reflects face, So a man's heart reveals the man." Proverbs 27:19

In other words, you should be able to look at a man's heart, as though you are looking into a pool and seeing your own reflection looking back at you. I can only say, this is not always a pretty picture. Amen

Jealousy and envy are spirits of complaining and murmuring.

"[Rebellious Korah and his followers envied Moses' leadership position and spoke against him, falsely accusing him:] And they gathered themselves together against Moses and against Aaron, and said unto them, Ye take too much upon you, seeing all the congregation are holy, every one of them, and the Lord is among them: wherefore then lift ye up yourselves above the congregation of the Lord?"

Numbers 16:3

Jealousy and envy are products of our carnal hearts.

"A sound heart is life to the body; but envy is rottenness to the bones."

Proverbs 14:30

I didn't say this; the Word of God states it so, in other words, a sound heart is life having everything we need in full within the body, energy, right standing in our spirits, and the breath of life in our minds and spirits. But yet, having envy, jealousy, resentment, hatred, malice deteriorates your being. It deteriorates who you are as a person and your feelings. You are looking good on the outside, but if someone would cut you open, split you in half, there would be rottenness to the core of your soul......Lord have mercy. So many are still walking in carnality, but there are some of us who would love to help.

Jealousy and envy provide the motivation for wrongdoing. We all know the story of David and Saul. Saul did not like David. In ***1 Samuel 18:1-7*** it speaks of Saul sending David out to war against the Philistines and wherever David went for Saul, he behaved wisely. However, on his return from warring with the Philistines, the women begin singing, dancing and playing music saying: *Saul had slain his thousands, and David his ten thousands.*

"Saul was the king, and he did not like the women singing this song because He hated David."

"So then Saul eyed David *from that day forward. And it happened on the next day that the distressing spirit from God came upon Saul, and he prophesied inside the house."*

1 Samuel 18:9

Further in the scriptures, it states that David was playing music and Saul was eyeing him from the room and threw a spear at David, but David moved out of the way of the, spear and it missed him......People of God, Saul was trying to kill David.

Eyed David, You may say that Saul watched David constantly, but we can't forget the eye someone may give you when they don't like you; cold, vicious eyes, that say "I want you to have your last breath." Some of you know exactly what I mean.

I mean it when I said "They want you to have your last breath." The Holy Spirit revealed that to me one day exactly as I stated. As I was sitting on a person's couch, suddenly spirits arose and attacked me; however, the Holy Spirit guided me thru the process. Simultaneously, while Guiding me, the Holy Spirit said, "they have sat on the couch, and thought of, and talked about your demise." I believe that was the first time I had ever entertained the word demise at any level.

The Holy Spirit then had me turn around several times with my prayer shawl, and begin to walk throughout the home with my Bible as He revealed the scriptures to me, and I recited them aloud for Him:

"Put away from you a deceitful mouth, And put perverse lips far from you. Let your eyes look straight ahead, And your eyelids look right before you, Ponder the path of your feet, And let all your words be established. Do not turn to the right or the left; Remove your foot from evil."

Proverbs 4:24-27

The important places the spirits raised themselves was in the area of the couch where the person often sat, and at the top portion of the bed in the bedroom. As I walked throughout the house, the areas of the scriptures where the spirits manifested were in verses 24 and 27. The words that should be noted are: "deceitful mouth and perverse lips.

1) Deceitful mouth is a "fruit" of the stronghold Spirit of Lying
2) Perverse lips is a "fruit" of the stronghold Spirit of Perverseness

It is important for you to see how devastating some unclean spirits can be, and jealousy, deceitfulness and perverseness are some of the worst to encounter. I believe jealousy is also one of the most prevalent unclean spirits that spreads itself so thin among the saved and unsaved. The scripture here also demands us to have perfected speech, for our eyes to look straight ahead, and to have the right walk with God. Allow your words to be established through Him, walk straight ahead, and remove your foot from evil ways.

On one occasion, someone had given me a compliment at work regarding a task I had done; after everyone left the area, one of the women got up and swept through the work I had completed, and all the documents fell to the floor. I shouted "what are you doing" as she ran back to her desk like a child and sat down in her chair with her hands overlapped in her lap. As the Holy Spirit opened my spiritual eyes, I saw her as a child being chastised by her mom whenever she was mischievous, and spanking her hands as well. I ran to her and said, "Give me your hands and playfully spanked her hands. She looked at me with rage and pain in her eyes." However, the incident was more serious than I actually played off, because I knew this person had so much jealousy inside her heart for me, and her anger and rage had surfaced. There were so many times she had shown signs of jealousy toward me. Jealousy is a nasty unclean spirit that is very dangerous.

Once upon a time, I acknowledged others jealousy, intimidation, and appeased their behavior toward me, but no longer. I now have compassion for those who are hurting inside and at times want to help them get through the pain.

Again, if you have an Anointing on your life, believe that at some point in time, someone will be jealous of that anointing. Remember, an anointing is given by God Himself; you have absolutely nothing to do with that. So be grateful, understand the will of God on your life, and walk in it.

During this period of time, the Holy Spirit truly began to orchestrate my life as He previously told me. He was also teaching me the kind of ministry I was walking into. I was absolutely amazed.

Notes to Myself

22

Reflecting

What an awesome and amazing God we serve. When the Holy Spirit begins to enlighten you about the things going on around you, and increases your knowledge regarding your walk with Him, that is an awakening. The truth will set you free; and when you learn about the things of God, and how He works in your life, there is no better freedom than that. The word states:

"For my thoughts are not your thoughts, nor are your ways My ways," says the Lord. For as the heavens are higher than the earth, so are My ways higher than your ways, And My thoughts than your thoughts."

Isaiah 55:8-9

My thoughts and my ways are higher than yours. I remember the first time I received a revelation about these scriptures; it was so awesome. I thought about how much larger Yahweh is than you and me, larger than anything or anyone I can imagine. I thought about my five-foot-one inch in height, and realized that no matter how huge my way of thinking was, I would have to go outside of the box on a massive scale. I was on a mission to learn.

When sent on assignments by God, at times I was not knowledgeable about who I was going to meet, and all the particulars for that assignment; however, the Holy Spirit guided me when the time came for every encounter, and gave me the ability to handle all the situations that occurred during those times. In due time, I would eventually know the assignment I was on. Remember, He doesn't send you out being unknowledgeable about the entire journey, because He will prepare you for what is to come.

The journey is not just for others, but you as well. The Holy Spirit is always teaching, instructing and giving directions for future assignments you will complete for Him. Regardless of the instructions from Him, just go. Don't worry about tomorrow, or how you may be feeling, or what to expect, or what you think you know and do not know. This is a plan of God's, not yours. Whatever and whomever you will encounter, God already has it worked out. Good, bad or indifferent. He is in it, and all you need to do is "walk in it."

"Consider the work of God; For who can make straight what He has made crooked? In the day of prosperity be joyful; But in the day of adversity consider; Surely God has appointed the one as well as the other, So that man can find out nothing that will come after him."

Eccelesiastes 7:13-14

Surely the word is letting you know that God is the God of adversity, as well as, the God of prosperity. Therefore, during your afflictions and adversities, know that they both come from the hand of God, and you should give thanks in times of prosperity. In times of adversity reflect on the goodness, and develop wisdom and understanding of the plan of God.

Some of you will definitely encounter jezebel spirits; they are everywhere. Remember jezebel spirits have mean, cunning and nasty spirits. Expect anything that is not like God to materialize in any given moment, and they always, always use other people to accomplish their goals.

Notes to Myself

23
Jezebel the Mastermind

Later I was employed at a service oriented business where I was able to minister to many hurting people for a while. Ministering to the assigned people was my assignment from the Lord, but I went through hell on the other hand with some of my colleagues. When you have a heart of a minister, it's very easy when people are sitting directly in front of you. People know real compassion when they see it. The services provided were for hurting people who had, and was enduring great loss and hardships during this timeframe. From the very beginning of this assignment the nasty, unclean spirits began to shadow me. I didn't allow this to stop me, because I realized my position was not just a "job," but on the flipside, "an assignment by God." My boss is God; therefore, I had to walk it out. Periodically, one of the managers would come to get me to attend to a client that was perhaps a little unruly, and an unclean spirit was manifesting itself, but before leaving the facility, all was well. This was a manager who did not walk in fear, and cared about the people.

From the onset of this journey, God began to show me who my enemies were, all types, sizes, colors, and levels. Aha, I supposed this meant I was going to really sink my feet into this one. During the prior years, I was unaware of the names of the unclean spirits that sought after my life, but this time, I was dealing with a whole new mind-set.

God had been training, guiding and directing me throughout the years, and every place I needed to go in order for my mind-set to be transformed and renewed. I now had more knowledge, wisdom, and understanding of the works of the enemy. Hallelujah to His Mighty and precious name.

There is nothing like a true awakening of God. When He gives you the gifts to see the enemy, hear the enemy, understand the enemies plots, know their hearts, and their abrasive schemes to use others to accomplish their plots against you, the only thing you can do is roll with the flow. They're going to come against you in several different angles, and this is where you will have to increase your time of being in the presence of God. You will still need His direction and instructions in this matter. It will be painful, but you cannot faint. The word states:

"He who plots to do evil, Will be called a schemer."

Proverbs 24:8

"If you faint in the day of adversity; Your strength is small."

Proverbs 24:10

Many will not understand your walk with the Lord; however, as long as you understand and use wisdom, in making your moves, God will be there for you. During this time, I endured many months of being harassed, targeted, while working in a hostile environment. I was surrounded by evil, insecure spirits, massive jealousies, and unforgiveness in all areas. Sometimes the atmosphere was like a time bomb waiting to explode. I had to deal with controlling, haughtiness, deceptive spirits, lying, spirits of intimidation, and spirits of heaviness.

Believe me when I tell you that I was growled at like a dog; I was told they were going to steal my joy, my work was retraced so that it would look as though I was making mistakes to cover their mistakes, my name was removed from documents when I found others errors, and once I mentioned to one of the supervisor's that she was mean to me; she alluded to the fact that others were no longer there because they said the same thing. I was stalked by an employee, and the manager's did nothing about it until the woman stalked a supervisor, then she was terminated.

Standing in front of several other employees, a supervisor stated, "I see documents coming through with Mary's stamp on them, and I'm wondering if I should put them on my bathroom wall." Needless to say, I was not shocked at this person's behavior because I realized he had a somewhat misguided and inappropriate personality that trickled from his mouth sometimes. I stated, "Yes, why don't you put the documents on your bathroom wall, many people read in the bathroom." Then, I walked away from him, and he said nothing.

I can't forget the supervisor that told me to come to a conference room, and when we got there the room was filled with clients. As we entered the room, he thrust the speech into my hands and ran out of the room and closed the door. When I realized what he had done, I didn't make a fool of myself as he obviously wanted me to do, but instead, I introduced myself and continued with the orientation process advising the clients of the procedures. I am acknowledging this because at the time it was not part of my responsibility to exercise that task. However, he did it because he thought it was going to embarrass me; but, the opposite occurred. Although he was my supervisor, I couldn't resist saying to him, "When you thrust someone into a situation like that, perhaps you should know something about their background. If you ever need a speaker, depending on the type of event, please let me know." I am not intimidated by crowds. I realized from all the things this person did against me, he hated me to the point that I felt sorry for him.

I had to daily deal with spirits that came at me as cunning lying spirits. They belittled me, displayed intimidation tactics, plotted against me, outbursts of rage, anger and conspired against me. The problem with unclean spirits is you never know how they're going to act or react to situations and circumstances. At any moment, hell can break lose all around you. Here are other encounters I had to endure while I was there:

There was an employee that would stand over my desk, look down at me, (threatening position) and whisper things she didn't want others to hear. I got tired of her doing that to me, and I finally rebuked her. As I spoke to the legions (unclean spirits), she fell out of her chair. Legions are in operation when there are many unclean spirits manifesting themselves.

In this situation, included are the major strongholds (lid spirits) that were operating in these situations.:

a) Stronghold Spirits of Haughtiness, Stronghold Spirits of Lying, Stronghold Spirits of Jealousy, the Stronghold Spirits of Fear and the Stronghold Spirits of Whoredom.

Recall the movie "Passion of Christ" and the Bible scriptures alluding to what I am going to say: "Remember when the devil was lurking in the Garden of Gethsemane as Jesus was nearing His death, Satan tried to tempt Jesus; now recall when He was on the mountaintop and was fasting for forty days, Satan tried to tempt Jesus, and even while Jesus was in the court yard being beaten to near death, Satan was still lurking and waiting for Jesus to give up." This is what jezebel masterminds do. They know your strengths and your weaknesses, and once they have you under their thumb, they move in on your weaknesses. The jezebel masterminds always remain behind the scenes, never confronting anything except through those they can manipulate and control. It's a sad situation when the jezebel mastermind is supposed to be intelligent, and they use their position, strengths and knowledge to try and destroy their employees and the victim. Unfortunately, some people are so easy to mislead. And, it's also sad because some people have very deep rooted issues they've been carrying for a long time.

I mention destroy the employees because if you are a supervisor who has twenty plus more years to work in the marketplace; and you are just learning to be a supervisor; there is a strong possibility that you will try to use the negative behavior patterns of your first supervisory position and the misguided knowledge you have been taught at other jobs. You should be cognizant that all organizations and managers do not use retaliatory tactics to teach and manipulate their supervisors, and to destroy other employees. Lord, have mercy. To think that your manager will have you purposely lie to one of your employees, knowing that it was going to backfire, was absolutely amazing to me. I felt really bad for myself once I learned of this, but I believe I felt bad for her as well, knowing how she was being taught to be a supervisor. There is no doubt in this life that what goes around, comes around. At some point in time, God reminds people of the seeds they have sown.

Later on, I approached the woman who had interest in what I was going to do for the rest of my life; and asked her, "Why did you come to my desk and ask me that question?" I will only tell you that suddenly I saw bulging red eyes, and facial expressions that were mean and distorted, as she said, "You always come to me as if I have motives for what I do and say." I stated, "Perhaps that is your perception." I wanted to say, "Stop allowing others to use you for their own good." Again, the devil will use you for his own selfish reasons, and all because he knows your weaknesses. How sad is it that a manager would do this to their employees?

God has certain assignments for all whom He has called; however, some of them are not very pleasant to walk into. All you need to do is remember some of the assignments and mandates given to prophets and priests like Ezekiel, Hosea, Jeremiah and many more, and you will understand that God is always helping His people, but someone has to be the underdog and walk the plan out. He will give us the strength, and His might to get through it all. If you lie to others, you will definitely lie to yourself. And when you encounter many lies from the same person, that person is walking in the "strongholds of lying spirits."

As you can see, one of the major ways to sabotage a person is to set up conspiracies. Manipulating other employees to go against you is one of the major ways "schemers" will use to get rid of you as well. Many of the people who go along with this process have things to gain, such as, not fearing the loss of their jobs because they helped Mr. Boss out, they are now more than ever in the boss's good graces, and hopefully, a promotion will happen at some point in time.

We cannot forget "retaliation." Retaliation is an act of payback, retribution, or revenge. Retaliation usually occurs if perhaps you filed a complaint against a supervisor (s). Although, they try to justify looking out for your best interest, trust me, stick around and watch the entire show. The company can't make it look as though they are retaliating; however, you know they are, but one way they can get revenge is via your performance.

Listed below is information I retrieved from the EEOC website regarding retaliation, and it will show you exactly why some employers will now come after employees they want to get rid of with other tactics:

Retaliation and Work Situations

The law forbids retaliation when it comes to any aspect of employment, including hiring, firing, pay, job assignments, promotions, layoff, training, fringe benefits, and any other term or condition of employment. http://www.eeoc.gov/laws/types/retaliation.cfm

The one thing some may not realize is that if they plotted against you, it can be done against them as well. You have to be careful when trying to hurt other people, especially when God has ordained them for the assignment. But, then they would not have known that God had anything to do with me being at that place, and even if they did, they would not acknowledge it.

One of the most important things I realized during that assignment is that the economy is so bad, and people will do anything to get you removed from your position if it means them progressing, or keeping their position. On the other hand, some people are just fearful of losing what they have, and are very mean-spirited as well. Fear is a very large part of your demise if you ever find yourself in these types of situations.

To get to my demise, I went through months of being harassed by one of my supervisors, and it was amazing the things Tom would go through to make me look bad. However, the tactics used was not working except into the hands of the bosses higher than us, whom also wanted me gone. There was no consideration on my part for the harassment I encountered, and the lack thereof. Many times I went into the office being a bearer of bad news on this person, until finally the head boss said "if you too do this again, I am going to fire both of you." With that statement, now I was being victimized twice. He knew that, but all this was part of the conspiracy. You see, the jezebel mastermind did not like me either. You know a leader is very angry when he/she adds verbiage onto their statements when introducing you, and the verbiage is unbecoming for a manager.

From the beginning, a jealous hearted woman named Busy Body lied on me to a manager, and stated that I said something about him, regarding his lack of knowledge for the work we were doing. The Lord revealed this to me when the manager came to me and stated, "if I wanted to tell him something, I could do it then." I instantly said, "I don't have anything to tell you." I never said anything to him about it; however, he walked around with the heart of hatred toward me for many months, and at times, spoke and displayed his feelings outwardly toward me. The lie she told him was obviously very painful, because he could not leave it to rest. He was determined to get rid of me; while he said, and did things at times, that was absolutely out of character for a manager. I understood his heart, but it was sad because he trusted and believed the word of the person that had lied to him. His heart was festering like a sore inside, and it caused his pain and anger to manifest into unclean spirits. I had never worked with this man one-on-one, so how would I know anything about his knowledge of what we were doing; however, he had worked with the person that lied on me. One thing I can be sure of is that God knows, sees and hears all things.

People of God these are the kinds of things that set you up in your workplaces. Liars are very sneaky and unsettled souls, who seek unclean means to destroy another person (s). I remember a T.D. Jakes sermon I was listening to a few years ago, and he stated, "Some of you are working with devils on your jobs that seek to devour you." He was so right. Don't kill the messenger if I got my verbiage confused on this statement; however, I was being devoured by some of my former employees during that time frame.

Lies, Lies, Lies – they can go on for days, months and years if no one stops them. I remember a quote that says, "Any lie told long enough, will eventually become the truth." The spirit of the Lord had advised me of the deceptive measures that were being planted against me. I am a very visual person, and when Busy Body would come to my desk, look down at me, and say things under her breath; I would see the devil as in the Garden of Gethsemane with the black cloak covering his head and face, sneaking around trying to disguise himself. The devil has a very sneaky spirit. The worst is that the leaders played into this kind of nonsense. Listed below is a scripture that speaks of the places I've worked at because they all eventually used other employees to conspire against me:

If a ruler pays attention to lies; all his servants become wicked.

Proverbs 29:12

My God, this scripture is so true because when you turn against someone who has done nothing against you to satisfy the satiable appetite of the wicked, you become wicked yourself. This is exactly what jezebel masterminds do to their employees, make them wicked. Don't blame me, as you can see, the word states it.

God knows all things. He knew who would like me; He knew who all my enemies were going to be before I entered the place, and He had it all planned out for the benefit of others and to glorify Him. If He didn't believe that I could handle this assignment, He would have sent someone else. However, I was the chosen one. I can only say that much greater is in store, and I passed the test, fore the Holy Spirit advised me of that as well after it was all over. My Father obviously trust me because He gives me some tough assignments. And, I still say "Yes Lord."

I was faced with acts of jealousy and outrage, harboring feelings that had not been dealt with from childhood, such as, tantrums, pouting, running away, retaliating against me whenever I found mistakes made by one of them, running to the head boss to tell more lies on me, emails being sent against me, and more lies to boot. I know we all make mistakes at work, but who dwells on them to the point of wanting to hurt another person? Here's a big one, never wanting me to be right, to the point of trying to really discredit anything that I did right to make me look wrong. Secondly, showing signs of jealousy whenever I was complimented for whatever the reasons were. These problems would increase over time.

Here's another thing, have any of you ever been in situations whereby someone will say something, good, bad or indifferent, but if you only "grunt" your name becomes mud. Welcome to the "out-cast club." Some people can say and do anything, while others can "grunt" and be stoned as if no one else has sinned. My Lord. You must have tough skin for God to use you in these types of situations. I am honored that He chose me for such a time as this. I believe this is another way Yahweh teaches you how to "stand alone."

I will say this, if you bring a complaint against one of your supervisors, your life will never be the same in that place. I did just that finally after being abused for months. Trust me, my write up was on point, and I told the truth and nothing but the truth; which put the leaders into a frenzy to get rid of me. I knew I was out of there so I may as well let them know how I viewed all of them. You may have been told that you should document everything, and that is true; however, if you need to show your documentation, then it's only a matter of time before your last day. Although they have documentation against you as well, they don't like it when you expose their hand.

Eventually, the human resources department and the leaders in your department will begin to conspire against you, secretly. It happens all the time. It usually does not matter what the "bad" supervisor has done against you, but your demise now has a shorter time period. Tom, one of my supervisors was working at another location for a few days, and Fancy, a supervisor tried to entice me to bring forth the documentation I had against Tom before he returned. I asked her "Why are you trying to get me to move on this, and why do you want him fired?" She became very inhibited and said "I thought because of all the things he's done against you." This is just a perfect example to show no one is trust worthy, and there is no loyalty.

In this case, the supervisor had harassed and targeted me for many months, while I worked in a hostile environment. Nothing seemed to stop this person. I tried coming to work and speaking directly to him only if it was absolutely necessary; and that occurred when my work needed to be reviewed. Whenever there was a quiet time, and hopefully things seemed to be getting better; he would come through like an unruly wind storm without a resting place. I then begin to analyze the behavior patterns of this person. I'd listened to one of John Maxwell's teachings on leadership, and he calls this kind of behavior from a supposedly supervisor or manager "A Momentum Breaker." A person that makes having a good day turn into a nightmare. "Lord, what was going on that had him so rattled that he couldn't compose himself?" The only thing that needed to occur was for me to find errors in his work. This made him go completely over the edge; even to the point of attacking me when clients were in the area. The only thing I could think of was he needed deliverance from traumatic experiences he obviously endured from childhood, or years prior to the current, because at that time the unclean spirits were manifesting. People of God, this is what happens when we travel through life and hold onto unforgiveness, shame, anger, and all that pain resides in our hearts for years. Suddenly without warning, outburst of anger, screaming, and shouting, spews out of the mouth.

Now another thing happens when a person has misplaced anger and aggression. They will sometimes implicate you in a situation as if there was direct correlation to something that may have occurred in their life in the past. This is "cause and effect." ***Meaning**: The one, such as a person, event, or condition, that is responsible for an action or result. Thefreedictionary.com*

***Aggression:** In such scapegoating, aggression may be displaced onto people with little or no connection with what is causing anger.*

***Transferential displacement**: The displacement of feelings and attitudes from past significant others onto the present-day analyst constitutes a central aspect of the transference, particularly in the case of the neurotic.*

Example: He stated to me that he had been criticized and chastised about his work; however, he was trying to make it seem as though I was unqualified in doing my work by associating himself with me. Then, he asked me what we should do about this? (transferential displacement). I was shocked; however, I told him that I wasn't going to do anything about this because I was not doing anything under handed, and whatever he was doing against me was his heart issues, not mind. Of course, I was called into the office and chastised, and written up for making the statement.

As he stated, his supervision knew his work habits, and although they had confronted him about this many times, they only covered it up in the end, and eventually used him to help get me out of there. But, as mentioned earlier, there is always more than one. The jezebel masterminds always have meetings behind your back, and get all your colleagues involved to prove their case. But, I stood the test of time.

I had another situation where one of my supervisors lied to me about one of the procedures of my work assignment, and that eventually caused me to be chastised and belittled by one of my coworkers that walked in **a Spirit of Haughtiness**. I tried to get the supervisor to make the lie right; however, my request was refused. I've been in a supervisor's role in the past, and had employees work for me; however, I never lied on any of them. That was very baffling for me at the time; however, lying spirits were on the rise.

Through all this and more, there is always one that will pretend to be your friend, but is really your arch enemy. These are the people who claim the name Jesus, Jesus, Jesus, while sticking a knife in your throat. Darkness cannot live in light, and light cannot live in darkness. Remember, these people are always hollering they are Christians; but I say now, obviously, they are not "remnants." Remnants of God don't take short cuts in and around the things of God. They walk in His will and His way all the time.

As John bore witness to the word of God, and to the testimony of Jesus Christ, to all things that he saw, John wrote these words as Jesus would speak to the Laodicea church:

"I know your works, that you are neither cold nor hot; I could wish you were cold or hot, So then, because you are lukewarm and neither cold nor hot, I will vomit you out of My mouth."

Revelations 3:15-16

Being a lukewarm Christian is not a good place to be in according to Jesus.

My performance was always very good, but one of the ways a company can cast you out is via your performance. Earlier in this topic, I mentioned that they never wanted me to be right to the point of trying to really kill anything that I did right to make me look wrong." This problem would become deeper. Therefore, to get rid of me, they had to do some of the most unethical things done in the workplace.

They began to make changes in the rules of my responsibilities and used other employees to help support their efforts; this made their lies support their case against me. Making changes in the rules of my work procedures was done by changing the rules so that when I walked into a meeting, I had not been updated on the new procedures, and then they lied when confronted on the issues. There were changes to what I could and could not say to a client, or perhaps not saying anything at all. Now, as far as they were concerned, I was now doing everything I was not supposed to be doing, and it was all incorrect. Does this sound familiar? The word speaks of twisting God's words. Well, believe me when you're in this kind of sewer, conversations, words, and behaviors all get twisted over and over again, and it's not in your favor.

Different procedures of the same task were being told to me than to my colleagues, although we had been doing this job for approximately six months. Now, everything was changing because I was in a different area. Different levels, different devils. This was part of the plan to have me removed, and having me separated from everyone else helped their purpose. However, God showed me everything they were doing, and having the ability to understand their underhanded methods. No one can beat God's giving.

Then, they brought in other management persons who would support their efforts, to lie about the warning they had given me, and bam, I was out of the door. Their mission accomplished.

Retaliation becomes a major part of your demise if you're ever in this type of situation. Because a company cannot file a Retaliation complaint against you, they will then challenge your performance.

Next is your character; Lord, help you if you're the type of person who hates petty nonsense, and of course, if God has given you the gift of discernment. Your discernment and walking in God's will can make it very difficult for you to put up with all the lying spirits, the backstabbers, and all the other unclean spirits you have to deal with on a daily basis. Walking in truth becomes a challenge; because you're probably the only one who is walking in truth. Those who are trying to dispose of your body in the workplace are certainly not walking in truth.

Now, if I didn't know who Yahweh is in my life, and if I didn't know His timing in my life, I probably would have been an emotional wreck as in previous years. But this time, the only pain I had was the disgusted feeling of knowing what was actually going on. While they were all creating my demise, the Lord showed me their moves. I was not walking in fear of anything because God gave me the ability to see and hear. I was assigned to a "room of isolation" after I made the complaint against one of my supervisors' and it didn't have a computer. They said the room was not wired for computers. At this point, who cares, because the scheming tactics were set.

Here's something else to look out for. There was another room next to my room of isolation, and they pretended one of my colleagues was going to occupy the room. He was in a state of confusion, and stated to me one day "they told me to come over here for at least an hour." This was the time and hour the human resource person was there, and they wanted it to seem as though they were not isolating me, because my colleague had an office next to me. Again, lies set up to convince the outside world that everything was perfect; however, it was not. I didn't really care because I knew my time was limited there, and I don't have a problem being alone. I know how to use my idle time. So they gave me more time to write. Thank you Lord for favor and the gifts you have given me.

When Yahweh turns up your gifting there is nothing anyone can do or say about it. Your job is to press into everything He is giving you. Actually while there, God increased one of my first gifts "administration," and that was so very obvious to many of my colleagues. Here's a definition of the gift of administration that I read in one of Chuck

Pierce's books, "Gift of administration is at the level that it links to the ability to oversee and direct others to execute responsibilities, with excellence and effectiveness." I had done this many times in this position, because when you use the Gifts that God has given you, they become very natural upon learning to walk in them. However, my actions became a threat to my supervisors. All hell broke loose around me. One of the funniest things I recognized was one of the supervisors always trying to prove his level of abilities to me. This was the same person who harassed me at his will. When a supervisor is threatened by your abilities, life can become hell in the workplace. Their spirits are always restless.

When you are walking in the will and way of God, your enemies have no idea they are helping you to accelerate to a higher level in God. They had no idea that God was using them to accomplish His great works, for me, to benefit others (including them) and to glorify God. As a matter of fact, most of them spoke the name Jesus or God; however, none of them actually lived the name of Jesus or God. Unfortunately, some of them didn't even like God. Case in point, anyone who calls you a "holy roller" does not like God. They're only repeating what they've heard someone else say, and they have no idea who God really is. Do you know that you know God?

Try this on for size. Has God ever used someone to bless you, and when they realized they really blessed you, they're not very happy about it? That's an awesome scene. God used a donkey, so why not you or your friends, family, or enemies? People of God, when the Father has His hands on a situation, believe me, He will show up and definitely make something out of nothing, and He will not allow that position to end until He's ready to do so. It was not my time to leave that place. God has His own timing. It took another five months before I was released.

With all the papers waiting in a folder ready to crucify me, and all the emails sent to end my life, God saw and heard it all. Unclean spirits are multiplying everywhere, and there are so many people that need to be healed. God is preparing His Remnant, for they are the ones who are mandated by God to do this great work of casting out unclean spirits, and calling in clean spirits.

When God exits you from a situation, don't look back, leave everything as it was, and keep it moving; or be like Lots wife and turn into a pillar of salt. As you continue to watch, you will see why God gave you an exit strategy.

During this season, I lived in a Stronghold world of lies, deception, jealousy, intimidation, haughtiness, fear, bondage and homosexuality. I was also stalked, and lied on by another woman; however, management did not do anything about her until she began stalking a supervisor. In the meantime, I was put on their outcast list, and labeled as not getting along with others. This is an opportunity for those of you who are now knowledgeable of these ways of life to understand that God does not want us to live in a bondage state of mind at any level; therefore, there are avenues to be free from this and all other unclean spirits.

Allow me to also say this "no one should have to downplay who they are to suffice for another person's insecure, intimidated feelings, or lack of supervisory skills." Unfortunately, for some of us, in the workplaces of today, you will probably be better off if you did not expose the knowledge, and abilities you have that far exceeds some of your supervisors. Some of today's employees are many light years away from 40 years ago. Obviously from my experiences of the past few years, you may need to come to work and melt in your seat while getting your work done, all in a day's work.

For current supervisors, because Jezebel's are on the rise; here's something for you to take notice of. Take notice of the supervisor who's always trying to get to know all your employees, while becoming your best friend. Jezebel spirits always have motives and intentions. This is food for thought for someone out there.

Now you have seen how "unclean spirits" affect our lives on a daily basis, and we all have them until you learn to cast them out. This is a process, and Jesus wants us all to be whole and fulfilled in our lives. However, there is a process before the casting out, which involves the revelations and clearing the pathway of the heart. You should not do one without the other.

For further assistance, my contact information is included on my informational page in the inside back cover of this book.

"Then He healed many who were sick with various diseases and, and cast out many demons; and he did not allow the demons to speak, because they knew him."

Mark 1:34

Notes to Myself

24

Exiting from Hell

Ironically, God put me in situations whereby I actually wanted, and He tried to help my enemies; however, they found this as a threat to them rather than a time of support. Walking in fear is like walking around with your eyes "shut wide." The devil has you blinded. Working in a hostile environment was heightened as the days continued.

During this time, the unclean spirits mannerisms had manifested to a level that I knew my end time was near. The mannerisms became more abrasive, challenging, and forthright. It had gotten so bad that one day I was reading John Maxwell's Leadership Bible and found something that I hoped would help, since everyone spoke of God from time to time. "Relationships: If You Get Along, They will Go Along." (Romans 12:9-21). I made copies of the information and gave to my supervisors, hoping this would bring some sense of peace. Actually, it only made them more hostile; however, they begin coming toward me like wolves in sheep's clothing, and pretending they were my friends. I knew better. I was trying to come to work and have some peace during the day.

You must speak when a person comes to work and targets you, and you are unaware why this is happening. In the prior years of conspiracies and sabotages against me, I did not speak because it was all unfamiliar to me, and I worked out of a complete outer-body experience.

So I probably inhaled a lot of anger. However, by the time the last episode occurred which was years later, I definitely stood firm on the things I believed in. The Holy Spirit had me in the Holy Spirit school of knowledge, wisdom, understanding, discernment, and revelation.

Walking with God and knowing His timing, is a process that Christians need to learn. It doesn't happen overnight, but again, it requires building a relationship with Him. My walk with the Lord requires me going on assignments for Him to expedite particular missions (sent one). Whenever you're working in ministry, there will always be someone to minister to; however, there will always be haters. You need to know how God works in your life. It's so very important.

People of God, if you don't know your seasons get up close and comfortable with the Father. Learn when your seasons begin, and end through Him. Sometimes, Yahweh does not tell you what your seasons are going to be like; just begin walking it out. I knew this season was over approximately a month prior to the end. As I was en route one day, the Spirit of the Lord spoke to me and said *"You have been in hell." I said, "Yes Father," and He said, "If Jesus had to go to hell, you had to also." I said, "Yes Father, and now you are bringing me out."* At that moment, I didn't know how it was going to end, but I knew it was not going to be pleasant under the circumstances. I was prepared for what was to come, and I accepted it, to move on with my life, and the next assignment. The only thing that made me a little upset was the lying. Living in a world with chronic liars is very annoying to me, particularly when I am the target. But then, the Father already knew these people before I did; He knew exactly what they were going to do, and so coming out of hell was an honor.

"For you have delivered my soul from death. Have you not kept my soul from falling, That I may walk before God In the light of the living?"

Psalm 55:13

I believe that if you are sincere about your walk with the Lord, be cognizant of those who are conspiring against you. I don't participate in festivities, eat their food, or take gifts from people I know do not have my best interest at heart. One of the individuals gave me a gift during the holidays, and I discarded it upon leaving the building. Many times other co-conspirators tried the same thing. I always returned the gifts. I will not receive gifts from people I know are trying to end my life. I know Jesus would not either.

Now the king of Sodom said to Abram, "Give me the persons, and take the goods for yourself." But Abram said to the king of Sodom "I have raised my hand to the Lord, God Most High, the Possessor of heaven and earth, that I will take nothing, from a thread to a sandal strap, and that I will not take anything that is yours, lest you should say, "I have made Abram rich."

Genesis 14:22-23

My sentiments exactly.

On the day of my termination, I was speaking to one of my colleagues, as she whispered that she too was going through some issues at work as well. I said to her, "perhaps we can tackle this together." She said, "oh no, you go on and do yours separately." I said, "Isn't it something that Christians can't stick together, but unsaved folk can?" As I walked away from her, the Lord spoke to me and said, *"Before the rooster crows three times, she will have denied you."* This statement refers to Matthew 26 when Jesus was speaking to the disciples.

Peter answered and said to Him, "Even if all are made to stumble because of You, I will never be made to stumble." Jesus said to him, "Assuredly, I say to you that this night, before the rooster crows, you will deny Me three times." Peter said to Him, "Even if I have to die with You, I will not deny You!" And so said all the disciples.

Matthew 26:32-35

Unfortunately, they all denied Him before that night was over. This is the way it is in ministry; sometimes you will stand alone. I Stand!

Honestly, I had not thought about those scriptures in quite some time; however; sometimes I am still at awe how quickly the Lord can brings things back to our remembrance. It amazes me how the Lord can keep us in the loop about all the things going on around us. The key is "relationship." If you do not have a relationship with the Lord, this is a great day to start.

I found this information to be quite interesting. On the day before I was terminated, my former supervisor asked me if I would go to another location to do some work, and I knew that I would have to work alone. It was raining so hard that one would have a hard time seeing objects in front of them. The other location was an hour away from where we were, and one and half hours away from my home. I reminded her that per the rules, we did have options to saying "no" when traveling to other locations. When she walked away, I thought to myself, "you want me to go to another location and work alone, but you don't think my performance is good enough here where I work every day." I knew that was part of the set up, and I definitely was not falling for it.

The next day, the supervisor came to me and said, "We are expecting a call from the human resources representative." The call finally came in much later in the day, and I was told that two days earlier I said something in a meeting that I should not have said, and so she would have to get back to me, and advise me of their decision. I reminded her that I have notes of the entire discussion we had three days prior, and none of what she stated to me was listed. Of course, she ignored my statement. Trust me, people of God, when someone is trying to destroy you, it's very unlikely that you're going to forget the conversation, particularly when you're writing notes. Believe me I am very good at keeping notes. None of this was true it was all part of the plan. And, when you are speaking to someone who is lying in your face, there is no need to bicker with them, because the lies are only going to escalate, and you're always going to be blamed for what is going on.

The explanation for the "performance issues in this case" actually had nothing to do with my performance. I was employed in a service environment, and I am a very compassionate person toward people. Therefore, I would occasionally ask clients if they understood specific information that was given or told to them, only if I saw or felt the need to. During the six months of working on the project, that was never an issue prior to, and during the harassment. All this happened after I made a claim against my supervisor who had been harassing me for six months. However, because I was now being retaliated against, they had to find reasons to get rid of me. Monitoring everything I said and did, became part of the daily responsibilities of my colleagues and managers.

The execution had a set day and time. Here's the key, God had a set day and time. How ironic that it was on Martin Luther King's birthday. As far as I was concerned, I was just set "free." The flip side to all this is that the government was coming in to take over the organization, and they wanted me out of there. One day there was a meeting at the location and one of the people directing the meeting had been to our location a few months earlier. I helped her complete the work assignment she had there; and when she returned a few months later, she began to look for me. Finally, after finding me, she said "I didn't remember your name, I've been looking for you, come with me." I told her my name, and she took me by my hand and we went to one of the conference rooms, and as we entered the room, it was filled to capacity, standing room only. She introduced me as the person who had taken the load off her shoulders and made her life so much easier to complete her task while she was there. Everyone congratulated me and gave me thanks. I turned and one of my manager's was standing next to me, but he never spoke a word. I returned to my desk and said "That woman just blessed my soul." One of my supervisors' said "How many people were in the room?" I gladly told her standing room only. Silence, you could hear a pin drop on the carpet. Jealousy at its best!

The Lord had already advised me that He was bringing me out of hell, and so it was done. It was approximately one month later after the

Lord spoke those words to me regarding my release from hell, and the termination was executed.

A few days after my termination as I was sitting and meditating, the Holy Spirit spoke and said *"There is no one left there that will stand by me."* **(emphasis)**. My heart was so saddened by His statement. He was right.

How many of us would stand for Jesus? The testing of many Christians faith will be coming very soon.

Notes to Myself

25

Divine Protection

Through the storms, battles, tornadoes, fights, and unclean spirits, you engage with on a daily basis, remember to seek God's protection during these troubled times. There are many scriptures that speak of God's divine protection and promises for believers. The word doesn't say your life is going to be easy; it's going to have wars, trials, tribulations, tests but He is going to be there even when He doesn't speak.

"For the eyes of the Lord run to and fro throughout the whole earth, to shew himself strong on behalf of them whose heart is perfect toward him. Herein thou hast done foolishly: therefore from henceforth thou shalt have wars."

2 Chronicles 16:9

Divine protection is the place where God has your angels surrounding you to protect you under circumstances that are beyond your reach. Some of these types of circumstances have been outlined in the previous chapters, especially when the enemy has risen to try to kill the works God has commanded. Others may be in relationships that are turbulent at times, and at that very moment when you feel you're at your wits' end, there is a move of God that only God can do to change that whole situation around. He is worthy; honor Him, worship Him, exalt Him, and lift Him up to show Him that you love Him like never before. Isaiah 59:19 is a great scripture to meditate on during an ugly scandal against you.

"So (as the result of the Messiah's intervention) they shall (reverently) fear the name of the Lord from the west, and His glory from the rising of the sun. When the enemy shall come in like a flood the Spirit of the Lord will lift up a standard against him and put him to flight (for He will come like a rushing stream which the breath of the Lord drives.)"

Isaiah 59:19

"Surely he shall deliver you from the snare of the fowler, And from the perilous pestilence."

Psalm 91:3

"Those who trust in the Lord are like Mount Zion, Which cannot be moved, but abides forever, As the mountains surround Jerusalem, So the Lord surrounds His people, From this time forth and forever."

Psalm 125:1-2

During all our trials and tests, we need to know that God fights our battles. He is our fortress, He is our defense, He is our hiding place, He is our rock, He is our refuge, and He is our shield. He is a divine keeper in everything we go through.

"The Lord will fight for you, and you shall hold your peace."

Exodus 14:15

Notes to Myself

26

God's Favored Ones

Being abused, misused, backstabbed, lied on, laughed at, left standing alone from time to time, abandoned, ridiculed and rejected. God's favored ones are the people who withstand the issues of pain, like Jesus did, and yet, become humble and love begins to ooze out of their veins, as they love those who have committed all kinds of sinful acts against them. No one but God can do that. And yet, He favors you.

It's complicated to imagine without going through trials and tribulations that you can be 'favored" by God and yet have to endure so much pain. But, as I think about Jesus, that's all I need to keep my head lifted up. We are favored by God, but we have to prove to Him that we can withstand the tests of time. We stand the test of shame, guilt, abuse, rejection and everything else that goes along with these issues. We must take a stand, and position that He has purposed and planned for our lives. We must go through all this to become that someone whom God needs to bring the lost souls to Christ, to travel far and near to reach the many people who are waiting to hear what the Lord has to say. We must go through all this while standing alone in areas that are filled with hatred, malice, jealousy, strife, and all the wiles of the enemy.

God's favored one is destined to help build His Kingdom and do great things for His Kingdom, and for the sons and daughters of God. It is His plan and purpose for His special people.

Notes to Myself

27

A Prayer for Your Soul

Because of His Favor

Most gracious and heavenly Father, in the name of Jesus, I thank you for giving me Favor over and beyond measure. I thank you for keeping me throughout all my trials and tribulations. Thank you for making me a beacon of light that you have encircled around me, and because of this light, mankind throughout the earth will become a lover of Jesus Christ our Savior, and will be brought to Him to be saved.

In the name of Jesus, you have protected me through the many years of my struggles, and now Father I have stood on your promises that I am now free to walk boldly before your throne of grace, and enter into your Holy of Holies. Thank you in the name of Jesus that my enemies have no rule over me and when they speak my name, Lord shut their mouths now and forever more.

In the name of Jesus, because of your favor, I have supernatural increase in every area of my life. I decree and declare that I have supernatural calling and promotions on my life through you, and others will be able to see the glory of the Lord upon me at all times. I declare and decree that I have financial increase in my hands and will lack nothing to do the work for the Kingdom. I prophesy, declare and decree through you O' Lord that there will be overflow in my storehouses, for your Kingdom. In the name of Jesus, I declare and decree that my health and my mind-set will remain healthy throughout the days of my life, and that there will be no hindrances in my life to continue my work for the Kingdom.

Heavenly Father, I declare that my financial cup spills over into the land, both near and far, and increases in areas that I have been in bondage for so long; and my assets are all set in place by you, and is being released from the land of poverty as I speak. I prophesy, declare and decree that every prison door that has had me in bondage is opened and I am passing through. In the name of Jesus, heavenly Father, I am most grateful and humbled for you allowing the Holy Spirit to be the orchestrator of my life, and directing me through this mandate that was preordained for my life.

Heavenly Father, I declare and decree that no good thing will be held from me. I will not lack anything that is needed for the Kingdom, and that I walk in spiritual wisdom, discernment, knowledge, understanding, the spirit of counsel, might, the fear reverence of the Lord, and the Holy Spirit. The spirit of the Almighty is upon me.

In all these things, I prophetically speak, declare, and decree that it is already done in the name of Jesus Christ our Savior.

Amen.

Notes to Myself

28

The Remnants

Yahweh is calling the remnant. Remnant means "survivor." If you have lived through the wilderness, been strengthened by God, called on by God, and are still living, I welcome you - you have survived.

The remnant was first brought forth by God with His promises to Abraham in Genesis 22. This was the time when Abraham had taken Isaac up to the mountain to present him to the Lord as a burnt offering. Because Abraham was obedient and he had begun to slay Isaac, the Angel of the Lord called to Abraham from heaven, and said:

And He said, Do not lay your hand on the lad, or do anything to him; for now I know that you fear God, since you have not withheld your son, your only son, from Me.

Genesis 22:12

We can see that one of the most important factors to becoming a remnant is being obedient to God. Being disobedient toward God leaves you in the same position as the Israelites in the past. He gives you time to learn to become obedient, but walking in His will and doing the things of God never change. God is not interested in whether you think His requests are right or wrong, or who His requests are slated for. He is only seeking a "Yes Lord" answer.

In various scriptures, you will find that God was always calling forth the remnant, restoring the remnant, and blessing the remnant. He did this because there were so many Israelites who were disobedient, murmured and complained about everything, and were never satisfied. Sometimes, we can't see the forest for the trees. Unfortunately, some people are so blind that they can't see that they're very blessed. Some have had very good jobs for many years, and only think of themselves, never blessing others unless they get a pat on the back. God sees everything.

The Lord was telling Isaiah to go and speak to the people; however, the Lord said, *"But yet a tenth will be in it, and will return and be for consuming, As a terebinth tree or as an oak, Whose stump remains when it is cut down, So the Holy Seed shall be its stump."*

Isaiah 6:13

We see here that the remnant is actually a small number of people. It's not surprising that the remnants are a small amount because we must be obedient to the will of God as **He** uses us for His glory, and we know that not everyone will always be obedient to God for one reason or another.

"There will be a highway for the remnant of His people Who will be left from Assyria, As it was for Israel In the day that he came up from the land of Eqypt."

Isaiah 11:16

God is opening up a highway right now for the remnant of His people. He is calling us in from near and far. It's stated in:

"And it shall come to pass in that day That the remnant of Israel, And such as have escaped of the house of Jacob, Will never again depend on him who defeated them, But will depend on the Lord, the Holy One of Israel, in truth."

Isaiah 10:20

Does anyone else feel as I do sometimes when I am reading and studying these scriptures, as if the scriptures are speaking directly to me? I can visualize myself in the place where I was surrounded by others who were not remnant, and in some way or another, they had defeated me. But now because I walk in the truth, I walk with God. I will do as He says; my power, boldness and authority has been raised to such a level that there is no longer any defeat in my life. God's got this and He trusts me as one of His remnant.

God has always been kind, loving toward His people, but their disobedience was always a problem. Therefore, your responses to God must be clear that you will represent Him in the way He wants, not your own ways.

As you read further in the word, (i.e., in Jeremiah, Isaiah, etc.) you will see that God always preserved the remnant – Why? Because God knows who He can trust to do His will. He knows that as a people we are going to be subjected to the issues of life. He knows that some people were going to be abused in all kinds of ways, beaten, emotionally scarred, neglected, rejected, abandoned, lied to, persecuted, living in fear, feeling insecure, hating others, and at times hating themselves. He knew many of us would live in some sort of sin and mankind would not forgive us, but we serve a loving God.

Through all our mess, God is the one who forgives like no other, and He knows the ones who will be so Grateful toward Him, that they will proclaim His name throughout the earth. He knows they will not care what the naysayers will have to say. He knows who He can trust, regardless of what these remnants are going through.

But, He also knows some of you have residue that you may not be aware of that is still lurking within your being from past hurts, stuff that is lying dormant in your subconscious mind, in your belly and heart, waiting to come out at an inopportune time. But God has a method for your problems to make you whole and go out into the world to help others become clean from their mess as well. Through the name of Jesus, we can cast out unclean spirits, (call out the strongholds and fruits) in your life, and call in clean spirits of God to live wholesome and free to do the things of God.

Those 7 Clean Spirits of God are as follows:

- The Spirit of the Lord Upon You
- The Spirit of Wisdom
- The Spirit of Understanding
- The Spirit of Counsel
- The Spirit of Might
- The Spirit of Knowledge
- The Fear of the Lord
- The Holy Spirit (bonus)

And the Spirit of the Lord shall rest upon him, the spirit of wisdom and understanding, the spirit of counsel and might, the spirit of knowledge and of the fear of the Lord.

Isaiah 11:2

Notes to Myself

29

Conclusion

"This is a mandate that was preordained by God, for your life to write this book," said the Lord on February 17, 2014, at 2:00 a.m. in the morning. I had been waiting thirteen years for Him to give me that message. I walked this journey out, I lived this journey, I cried and I lost so much, but somehow, I held on to Him. There was no other way for me to have written this book without living through the journey. I did not die, but was always steadfast to benefit others and to glorify God. Many years prior I had asked Him, "What was my purpose for being born?" Like so many other priests and prophets in the Bible, I, too, had a mandate and preordination on my life. He allowed the enemy to attack me in some very severe ways, but like Job, I held onto His promises and received the victory. Now, I live Him from the inside out.

My life has been on an awesome journey that I never would have expected, and I know there is much more to come. Actually, I was amazed to know when God began to call me into ministry years ago, and definitely when the Holy Spirit began training me for the call on my life. It's been an awesome experience that is continuing on a daily basis.

The Lord revealed to me just before completing this book that I walked in seven stronghold spirits and some of their "fruit" during the many years I was coming into ministry and before being saved. I am not ashamed to know this, and have no problem revealing this to my readers. If there is one thing we all must do in life is to be very honest with ourselves. Actually, I am glad to know this now, because I periodically check myself and begin to cast out, and call in the clean spirits of God. We all need to send the devil packing to those dark and arid places where he belongs, never to return again. When my Father revealed that to me, I cried knowing that I was a complete mess. I had so much compassion for myself about this as if I was feeling the pain for someone else.

Stronghold spirits and their fruit are in everyone at some point in time. They can manifest through and upon you on a daily basis. They can come through generational curses before you entered into your mother's womb, and can materialize from many types of relationships, pain of all sorts, and all the negative issues of life. But because of the name called Jesus our Savior, there is a way for us all to live "free." In the name of Jesus, cast out the stronghold spirits and their "fruit" from your life, and live a wholesome victorious Life in the name of Jesus. Know that God loves you very much, get filled with the Holy Spirit and allow Him to orchestrate your life.

"And He has filled him with the Spirit of God, in wisdom and understanding, in knowledge and all manner of workmanship."

Exodus 35:31

The Lord is bringing more and more life issues to our attention that He is unpleased about, and sabotaging his sons and daughters is one of those areas where His people suffer. God does this over and over again, having a call on someone's life that will help to strengthen His people, and bring situations and circumstances to the light. Many of His people suffer in areas that are unbelievable, and many times in silence, but we make it through. He cares for you, and all that you and your loved ones go through. He wants you all to live a healthy and wholesome life. He wants you to be free from hurt, harm, and danger.

Through our suffering, He makes a way to escape. Suffering is a road where many of us travel, but during that time, we are refined and sharpened in areas where we need it, so that when the suffering is over, we can teach others how to make it through and God will get the glory. We have a mighty job to do on this earth, because there are so many people who suffer in silence from all types of abuses and evil spirits, but again, when there's one that will teach another, God is well pleased.

"But the Lord said to him, "Go, for he is a chosen vessel of Mine to bear My name before Gentiles, kings, and the children of Israel. For I will show him how many things he must suffer for My name's sake."

Acts 9:15-16

Isn't it awesome as the Lord spoke to me and said "He had a mandate that was preordained for my life?" The most phenomenal mandate that was ever preordained for anyone's life was Jesus. His job was to come here on earth for a short time so that we might be saved from our sins, and He ultimately died for our sins. I did not die from the hardships I went through; however, I did learn how to live through Jesus and the teachings of the Holy Spirit. And I love teaching others about the Father, the Son, and the Holy Spirit.

I have offered references that may help you along the way if you're ever in some of the vicarious situations I have been in, just know that you too, can have a clean spirited life and filled with the Spirits of the Most High God. I assist others to become free of unclean spirits. My contact information is listed on the last page of this book.

Also, if you are ever in any type of plans regarding sabotage, conspiracies, harassments, targeting, or working in hostile environments at your workplace; please keep a journal of the issues that are attacking you from beginning to end. Document everything. Amen.

This book is my memoir, and as such, all facts and issues stated in this book happened to me personally, orchestrated by the Holy Spirit. No incidents in the book are meant to harm anyone, personally, spiritually, or otherwise, but to educate you about the abusive tactics people endure at the workplace. We all have issues in our lives, and therefore, people enter our space for many different reasons. All the encounters that were involved in my life was purposely orchestrated by the Holy Spirit to teach me more about the kind of ministry He was entrusting me with, to give others knowledge of the unclean and clean spirits we carry as a people, and the evils of sabotage that so many people experience in the workplace.

I am still a work in process and steadily progressing. However, our Heavenly Father has made a way for us all to be free from unclean spirits. This book is also a teaching tool for those who want to be "free" and those who want to really learn how to get into the presence of God. Depend on Him, trust Him, believe Him, worship Him, praise Him, and love Him. This is what He wants from all of us.

I have been mandated and preordained by God to write this book, live this life, and travel this journey, and "Now I Have the Best Job in the World" as a:

Kingdom Priest!

"Everything that looks like a loss, just may be an extraordinary successful life, waiting to explode!"

Mary V. Pate

"Thus says the Lord, your Redeemer, The Holy One of Israel, "I am the Lord your God, Who teaches you to profit, Who leads you By the way you should go."

Isaiah 48:16

Uncover My Heart

(A Prayer)

I have incorporated two prayers that you may find useful for yourself or others. Add the correct verbiage that applies to your own situations. Also, see the list above for the seven clean spirits of God to add into the verse below.

Father, in the name of Jesus, uncover my heart so that I may know who I am. Uncover my heart so that I may live and be free from all unclean spirits for you. Jesus, come into my secret place so that I may go into your most Holy place to talk with you, to sing with you, oh' Lord. Become my resting place. In my time of need, comfort me Holy Spirit, guide me in the way in which I should go, and protect me from my enemies. My heart belongs to you Father and every part thereof.

Satan, I take authority and dominion over my life, because this temple belongs to Jesus, and you have no authority over me. In the name of Jesus, Satan I demand you to go now to the dry and arid places and never return to my life again, never return to my dwelling place, and never return to my ministry, never touch my finances or my family. In the name of Jesus, every unclean spirit and its fruit that has rested within me is now gone, and I am filled with the seven spirits of the Most High God (**name the spirits you wish to call in**). Father, I trust that you will keep me in your grace and wrap me in your loving arms as you Uncover My Heart daily in Jesus mighty and precious name.......
Amen

Notes to Myself

Salvation

(A Prayer)

Father, in the name of Jesus, I come before you as humbly as I know how. Father, I have sinned before you many days of my life, and now I come with my mind, body, spirit, and soul before you and ask for your forgiveness, and to repent of my sins before you. I accept Jesus as my Lord and Savior to learn to walk in His will and His way.

In the name of Jesus through the Holy Spirit, teach me how to walk in the boldness, power, and authority as you have stated in Luke 10: 19. Teach me how to become humble toward you, teach me how to hear your voice, teach me how to live my life the way only you would like me to. Lord, fill me with the Holy Spirit, so that I may be used by you. Teach me how to tell others about you in the name of Jesus.

In the name of Jesus, thank you Father for saving me.

Amen.

About the Author

Mary V. Pate is after the heart of the Holy Spirit. The Lord launched her into ministry several years ago through the Holy Spirit's wilderness school after sixteen years of long suffering. She has the keen ability to hear the voice of God while allowing Him to orchestrate her life. She began her ministry focused on leading women's conferences, teleconferences, and workshops teaching the word of God on various topics that were led by the Holy Spirit, with instructions on how to apply the word of God directly to your life. The Lord has led Mary into the ministry of deliverance and healing. She walks in an Apostolic anointing, and is an author, certified life coach, inspirational/transformational speaker, conference leader, and kingdom trainer. She has written several books ordained by God to reach people globally, and continues to write words brought forth by the Holy Spirit.

Mary V. Pate's Ministry is committed to teaching others how to live victorious and successful life styles.

Selah!

Speaking Opportunities: Contact Info:
Email: mpateministries@gmail.com
www.MaryVPate.org

Published Books by Mary V. Pate

- Motives of the Heart through trials Tribulations and Tests
- 10 Powerful Keys to Letting Go: Living a Victorious Life (ebook)
- 8 Golden Rules: How to Move Yourself Out of the Way (ebook)
- Destiny Calling (coming in 2017)

www.ingramcontent.com/pod-product-compliance
Lightning Source LLC
Chambersburg PA
CBHW030934090426
42737CB00007B/427